# Mary's Vineyard

# Mary's Vineyard

## DAILY MEDITATIONS, READINGS, AND REVELATIONS

### Andrew Harvey & Eryk Hanut

A publication supported by
THE KERN FOUNDATION

### Quest Books
Theosophical Publishing House

Wheaton, Illinois ♦ Madras, India

*The Theosophical Publishing House*
*P.O. Box 270*
*Wheaton, IL 60189-0270*

*A publication of the Theosophical Publishing House,*
*a department of the Theosophical Society in America*

**Library of Congress Cataloging-in-Publication Data**

1/97

*Harvey, Andrew, 1952-*
    *Mary's vineyard : daily meditations, readings, and revelations / Andrew Harvey & Eryk Hanut.*
*— 1st Quest ed.*
        *p.       cm.*
*"A publication supported by the Kern Foundation."*
*"Quest books."*
*ISBN 0-8356-0745-3*
*1. Mary, Blessed Virgin, Saint—Hermetic interpretations.     2. Mary, Blessed Virgin,*
*Saint—Prayer-books and devotions—English.      3. Devotional calendars.*
*I. Hanut, Eryk, 1967-    .       II. Title.*
*BT605.4.H47H37    1996*
*232.91—dc20*
                                                                    *96-7868*
                                                                    *CIP*

8  7  6  5  4  3  2  1  *  96  97  98  99  00  01  02

*Book and Cover Design by Beth Hansen*
*Cover photograph by Eryk Hanut*

*This book was set in Galliard Italic, Trajan Demi, Skylark, Ovidius Demi, Lombardy, and Geometrica.*
*Printed in the United States of America.*

V

*For Helen McDermott,*
*who taught us the Hail Mary*
*in many more ways than she may believe.*

*A. H. and E. H.*

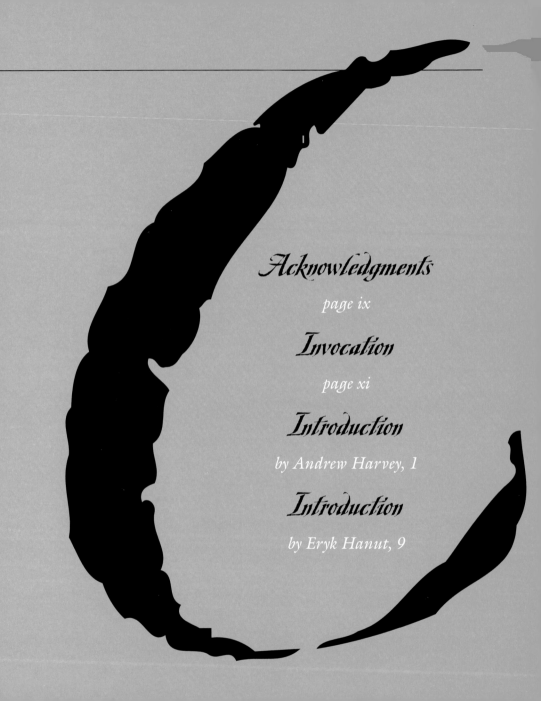

# Contents

# *Acknowledgments*

THANKS to Cynthia A. Cannell, agent of agents and precious friend; Brenda Rosen, for her sensitivity and doggedness; Sharon Dorr, for her enthusiasm and wonderful help; Leila and Henry Luce III for all their love.

A special thanks to Beth Hansen. Thank you, Beth, for your wonderful talent and the beauty of your work and your soul.

Thanks, too, to Mollie K. Corcoran, for the love and help she gives endlessly.

With loving gratitude to Michelle Ryan, Caroline Bouteraon, Sister Lucie from the Carmel of Mont/sur/Marchienne, Karen Kellejian, Catherine Laboure, Melanie Calvat, Maximin Giraud, Bernadette Soubirous, Jacinta Martos, Francisco Martos, Sister Lucia, Albert, Fernande, & Gilberte Voisin, Andrée & Gilberte Degeimbre, Mariette Beco, Sister Faustina, Estela Ruiz, Bernardo Martinez, Rosa Quattrini, Myrna Nazzour, Julia Kim, Father Stefano Gobbi, Vicka, Jakov, Mirjana, Ivanka, Marija, and Ivan—Visionaries of the Virgin, for their testimony.

*I saw such gladness rain down upon her*

*Carried in the holy minds*

*Created to fly through these heights*

*That everything I had seen before*

*Had not seized me with such wonder*

*Nor shown me such a likeness to God.*

DANTE, *Paradiso*, CANTO 32

*I salute you, Glorious Virgin, Star more brilliant than the Sun, redder than the freshest rose, whiter than any lily, higher in heaven than any of the Saints. The whole earth reveres you, accept my praise and come to my help. In the midst of your so glorious days in heaven, do not forget the miseries of this earth; turn your gaze of kindness on all those who suffer and struggle and never stop soaking their lips in the bitterness of this life. Have pity on those who loved each other and were torn apart. Have pity on the loneliness of the heart, on the feebleness of our faith, on the objects of our tenderness. Have pity on those who weep, on those who pray, on those who tremble. Give everyone peace and hopefulness. Amen.*

ANCIENT PRAYER OF PROTECTION CELEBRATED BY MYSTICS AND HEALERS

# Introduction

by Andrew Harvey

"Mary is the unrecognized Mother Goddess of Christianity."

ANNE BARING AND JULES CASHFORD, *THE MYTH OF THE GODDESS*

"I love you my little ones and I do not wish to see you destroy one another."

OUR LADY TO ESTELA RUIZ, PHOENIX, 1991

MANY seekers and lovers of God of all kinds and faiths are agreed that the single most important aspect of the spiritual life of the world today is that everywhere we are witnessing a return to the Mother, to the long-forgotten, long-derided Mother-aspect of God. For too long the major religions and mystical traditions have been biased towards transcendence and attached to detachment. This bias and this subtle attachment to a vision of the Divine that separates it and us from our bodies, our ordinary *lives, our sexuality, and Nature have, it is becoming clear, abetted the destruction of the planet and not worked to prevent it. Those who love the Mother know that unless we turn to her and allow her profound and passionate knowledge of interdependence and love-in-action at every level and in every dimension to penetrate, transform, inspire, and guide us—we will not find in ourselves the vision or passion or wisdom necessary to preserve the planet.*

*To a world ravaged by disunity, the Mother offers the revelation of oneness; to an age inwardly destroyed by apathy and anxiety, the Mother offers the grace of a holy and peaceful passion that blesses, loves, and protects all things and knows all things and beings as sacred emanations of a common source; to beings panicked by the threat of a worldwide ecological catastrophe, the Mother offers strength, hope, and the inner power to effect a change of heart, and the radical political and economic action that must follow such a change; to those depressed by the harshness of working for justice and transformation in so deluded and secretly devastated an age, the Mother offers her protection and her humble stamina and that force of unconditional love that is her essence and her gift and that no power can defeat.*

*In this worldwide return to the Mother and to the healing and invigorating wisdom of the Sacred Feminine, nothing is more significant or inspiring, especially for those brought up, however difficultly, in the Christian tradition, than the extraordinary attention being paid by seekers of all kinds to Mary. During the last 150 years, Mary has been appearing all over the world, delivering short simple messages of infinite love, wisdom, and urgency, trying to wake her children up to the enormity of the danger they are facing and to the remedies of prayer, mutual honor, and hard work in every dimension that alone can save the situation. Increasingly and for people of all faiths, Mary is being liberated from the golden cage of patriarchal adoration that has kept her prisoner for so long and is being revealed for what she is: the Divine Mother in full force and splendor, as essential to the working out of the Christian mystery as her Son—the most human of all the faces of the Mother, the one turned with most urgent and passionate love towards humankind.*

*Kali and Saraswati, Isis and Astarte, and the great Goddesses of South America and Africa are all marvelous cosmic revelations of the Mother. Mary has the power and range of all of these, but being also once human, it is clear to anyone devoted to her that she has a very personal interest in the world, a very anxious interest, one that emphasizes—as none of the other aspects of the Mother do with quite such intimacy or anguished passion—the glory of this world and the absolute necessity of doing everything in our power to preserve it.*

*Mary's message is a simple one: "Realize the essential unity in my Sacred Heart of everything that lives; ripen that knowledge and love through continual prayer; enact that knowledge in every aspect of life to irradiate life with my power, truth, tenderness, and passion for justice." All the old barriers between faiths, peoples, sexualities, castes must now be dissolved, for differences create division, and there is no more time left for the dubious luxury of divisiveness.*

*Mary knows, and makes clear again and again that she knows, that our situation is desperate, that evil is extremely powerful, and Nature—the body of the light—is in appalling danger. She knows that we cannot preserve ourselves unless we undergo a massive change of heart that leads to a commitment at every level to make love real in action and to implement justice in every arena. She knows that there are immense forces ranged against us, ranged against the success of the human enterprise.*

*Mary also knows that if we can turn to the Mother, to her mercy and her power and her love that live in us as our deepest identity and heart-truth, miracles of transformation are possible—miracles that are not simply personal and spiritual, but ones that effect the changes that will save the whales and the dolphins and Antarctica and Amazonia, as well as the future of the soul of every human being. Nothing is impossible to her children, if they recognize, honor, and pray to their Mother. Together with the Mother, we can still, even at this late hour, do anything.*

*"My Immaculate Heart will triumph," Mary said to the children at Fatima, after being terrifyingly clear about the dangers ahead. Mary's heart—and the heart of her Son—will triumph, but only if we all turn to them now, with humility and confidence and complete lack of illusion about the potentially terminal danger we are in.*

Eryk and I have made this book as an aid in this turning of the whole being towards her. Mary, our Mother, needs no elaborate address, no fancy meditations, no complex prayers. Saying her rosary and talking to her from a full heart are always enough, and she will answer every request directed to her, as everyone who risks intimacy with her knows beyond doubt. We have brought together here those prayers, meditations, and mystical insights culled from her greatest lovers over 2,000 years that have most intimately helped us in our longing to be closer to her and to realize her love in the world.

Weave the meditation we have given into your prayers, thoughts, and actions each day, and you will find, as we have, that your whole being will be strengthened in the fire of the Mother's hope and truth. And with that hope and that truth increasingly established in our hearts, minds, bodies, and souls, nothing will be impossible to us, her children.

The Virgin said to Sister Faustina in the 1930's, "Mankind will not have peace until it turns with trust to my mercy." To Father Stefano Gobbi, the Virgin said in 1987, "I am gathering my children from every part of the earth, and enclosing them in the refuge of my Immaculate Heart, so that they may be defended and saved by me, at the moment of the Great Trial which has now arrived for all. So, in the very years when evil is triumphing by leading humanity along the road of its own destruction, my maternal heart is also triumphing, as I bring my children along the

*way of salvation and peace." She added,
"My light will become stronger and stronger the more you enter into the decisive
moments of the battle."*

*This battle for the future of human-
ity is now raging in every field of human
life. Everything depends on the intensity
and the seriousness and the comprehensive-
ness with which we summon the Mother's
love and power, and enact it.*

*We pray that this book will furnish
all who come to it those arms of love, mystical trust, and insight that we all need, to
endure, to struggle calmly, and to win, in
her name and for her glory.*

*O Divine Mother, Save, Inspire,
Elevate, Stabilize, Humble, and Embolden
us all.*

*I dedicate this text to my mother,
Kathleen Elizabeth Harvey.*

# Introduction

*by Eryk Hanut*

O what's new? Mary. Mary is new. She is always new. I was, I have to admit, terrified of taking these photos. Terrified of "stealing" these images from the Divine Mother—who still, despite everything, let herself be invaded without forfeiting anything of her oceanic grace or of her smile.

It's a cliché to talk of "stolen images" when it comes to the work of photographers. All photographers talk like this. If they were as ashamed as they claim of "stealing," they would do another job.

But the interdiction is real. I felt it often, that "no, this moment does not belong to me". . .

Mary discourages thieves from "stealing" and encourages them to take freely. Her door is flung wide open. Everything is offered. The table is laid. Disturb Mary? The Mother of the Heavens? Do you "disturb" the sea when you fetch a bucket of water from it? For all the immensity that Mary is that would dizzy us if she weren't also total love, there is also—and this is her most tender miracle—intimacy with her. Intimacy. What an amazing word! Intimacy . . .

*Mary is gigantic, but also tiny and hunched with humility. Far but never, ever, distant. She is the bedside lamp we can switch on at any moment to dispel the darkness.*

*Mary draws millions to her, gives sight to the blind, makes springs gush at Banneux, Lourdes, La Salette. Mary made the sun dance at Fatima and a tree at Beauraing break into blossom in the middle of winter. She gives you what you would expect from a Queen—glory. But she also gives what you would hope from a Mother. Mary cooks the soup, squinting anxiously at the clock if her child is late.*

*Mary is the clock, but she is also the first to forget it. Everyone knows this who kneels and prays to her. She is there; she can do anything; she has been through everything. What could be more mind-shattering than the destiny of this tiny Jewish girl, this thirteen-year-old who said "yes" to the plans of God?*

*Everyone knows how tremendous Mary's destiny is. That is why anyone can ask anything from her. Everyone, on one day or another, has asked her for something—even those who are closed to her mystery.*

*I often ask myself if the adoration we give her matters to her at all. She wants our best. That is all that matters to her. She is the spare tire you don't think of hidden away in the trunk of the car. When you're driving across a desert and have a puncture, then, suddenly, that spare tire becomes overwhelmingly important.*

*Nothing is more poignant than a person who prays. To pray is to become a*

*little child again. It is to talk to your Mother without a grill between you. And the
Mother listens, consoles, replies . . .*

*As for Mary as "photographic subject," Cocteau said, "Fashion is what quickly
goes out of fashion." Mary can never go out of fashion, any more than the sun, or
trees, or love. She has not "returned." She has never been away. She has been waiting.
Her children can disguise her, give her other names. She just smiles. They can stop
believing in her altogether. She goes on believing in them. She waits. She arrives.*

*Mary, then—no, here it is a question of Marys—in aluminum forty feet high,
in porcelain, plaster, gold, wood, plastic. Marys from India, Marys from California,
from Peru, from France. Marys from towns, from cemeteries, from mountaintops.
Marys from Massachusetts and from Belgium.*

*Our Mother, which art in Heaven, your kingdom come. This book contains
only some of your words and faces. Thank you, Mother, for the opportunity to make
this book. Thank you for the intimacy. With or without this book, you, as your Son also
promised, are with us always, in all circumstances, until the end of time. Hail Mary,
full of grace.*

*I dedicate this text to my dear friend, Mary Ford-Grabowsky.*

# Mary, the Divine Mother

*Mary is increasingly being recognized not merely as the Mother of God or as the supreme intercessor between humankind and the Father, but as the Divine Mother herself, with the full powers of the Divine Mother. What my long journey into the sacred feminine has taught me and what my own inner experience of the grace of Mary has confirmed in me is that Mary is the Mother of the universe, the divine and human mother of us all. I believe that until the full majesty and grandeur of Mary's presence in the Christian revelation is understood and embraced, the full force of the Christian vision of Love-in-Action cannot be released. This is why I have dedicated the first month of the year to the "greatness" of Mary and of the Mother, whose most poignant and urgent face she is.*

# January

*All the powers of all the world's Mothers—Tara, Durga, Kali, of the Tao— are in Mary. She has Tara's sublime protectiveness towards all creation; Durga's (the Fortress's) inaccessible, silent face; the grandeur and terribleness of Kali; the infinite awareness of balance and mystery of the Tao. The miracle of Mary and the source of her extraordinary hold over the human heart, however, is that she was a human mother as well, a mother who endured every imaginable anguish and so shares all of our griefs with an intensity and an intimacy no purely Divine Mother can. In Mary, then, we have a complete image of the Divine Feminine, an image at once transcendent and immanent, other-worldly and this-worldly, mystical and practical.*

*It is this full and complete Mary that seekers of all kinds are turning to at this late and terrible moment to help transform their own lives and the world itself into a living mirror of the Love and Justice of the Mother.*

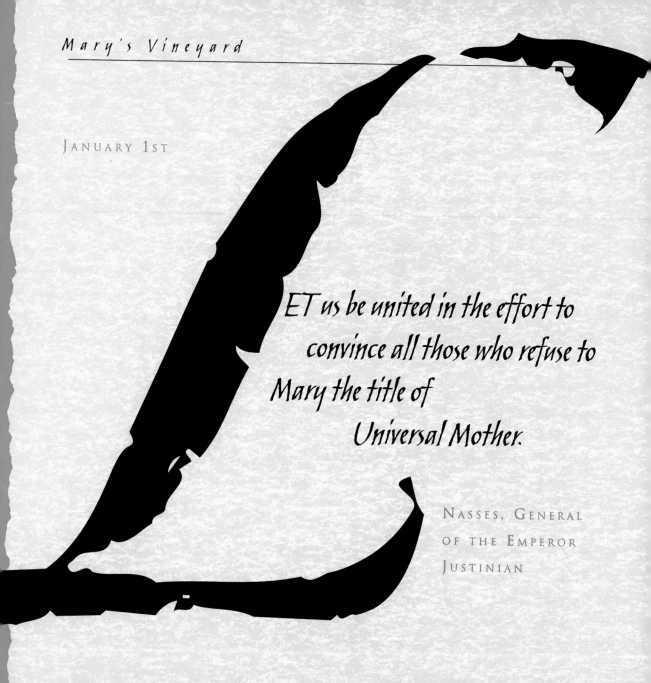

JANUARY 1ST

*ET us be united in the effort to convince all those who refuse to Mary the title of*

*Universal Mother.*

NASSES, GENERAL
OF THE EMPEROR
JUSTINIAN

## JANUARY 2ND

*With whom can we compare you, O Mother of grace and beauty? You are the Paradise of God. From you springs the fountain of living water that irrigates the whole earth.*

SAINT BERNARD OF CLAIRVAUX

## JANUARY 3RD

*Wishing to create an image of all beauty, and to manifest clearly to men and angels the power of his art, God created Mary all-beautiful. In her, God has brought together all the partial beauties which he distributed amongst other creatures, and has made her the ornament of all beings, visible and invisible; or, rather, God has made her a blending of all perfections—divine, angelic, and human; a sublime beauty that adorns two worlds, lifted up from earth to heaven, and even transcending that.*

GREGORY PALAMAS

## JANUARY 4TH

*The Eternal Father made her entire being radiate divinity; for since the divine word was to spring out of the breast of the Eternal Father to flow down to that of Mary, he provided for the most exact imaginable symmetry between the Mother and the Father.*

MARIE OF AGREDA

## JANUARY 5TH

*And there appeared a great sign in Heaven; a woman clothed with the sun, with the moon under her feet, and upon her head a crown of twelve stars: And she being with child cried, travailing in birth, and pained to be delivered.*

REVELATION 12:1–2

## JANUARY 6TH

*At the command of Mary, all obey—even God.*

SAINT BERNARDINE OF SIENNA

## JANUARY 7TH

*A single sigh from Mary has more power before God than the combined pleadings of all the saints.*

THE DEVIL TO SAINT DOMINIC

### January 8th

*The entire ancient world, from Asia Minor to the Nile and from Greece to the Indus Valley, abounds in figurines of the naked female form, in various attitudes of the all-supporting, all-including Goddess . . . and so it came to pass that, in the end and to our day, Mary, Queen of Martyrs, became the sole inheritor of all the names and forms, sorrows, joys, and consolations, of the Goddess-Mother in the Western world: Seat of Wisdom, Vessel of Honor, Mystical Rose, House of Gold, Gate of Heaven, Morning Star, Refuge of Sinners, Queen of Angels, Queen of Peace.*

Joseph Campbell

### January 9th

*These are the Virgin's names: a throne,*

*God's canopy,*

*Ark, fortress, tower, house, garden, mirror, fountain,*
*The sea, a star, the moon, the rose of dawn, a mountain:*
*She is another world, so can be all these things freely.*

Angelus Silesius

## JANUARY 10TH

*Lady, you are so great and so powerful,*
*That man who seeks grace and does not first seek you*
*Would have his prayer fly upward without wings.*

DANTE, PARADISO, PRAYER OF SAINT BERNARD, CANTO 33

## JANUARY 11TH

*If only a child can see your face / And count on your constant help / Unwind me*
*from these bonds of age / Make me again your little child / The innocent faith and*
*innocent love / Of golden childhood live in me still.*

NOVALIS

## JANUARY 12TH

*The Mother of God, since she gave her son the humanity of the second Adam, is also*
*the mother of universal humanity, the spiritual center of all creation, the heart of the*
*world. In her, creation is completely divinized, and conceives, fosters, and bears God.*

SERGEI BULGAKOV

### JANUARY 13TH

*I pray to the Divine Mother of God,*
*Heavenly Queen of all living things,*
*That she may grace me the pure light of the tiny animals*
*That have a single letter in their vocabulary.*

FEDERICO GARCIA LORCA

### JANUARY 14TH

*As wax melts before fire, so do all devils and evil beings lose their power against those*
*souls who often remember the name of Mary and passionately invoke it.*

SAINT BONAVENTURE

### JANUARY 15TH

*Before the birth of the Virgin, a constant flow of grace was lacking, because this*
*aqueduct did not exist.*

SAINT BERNARD OF CLAIRVAUX

### JANUARY 16TH

*Mary Immaculate, / Merely a woman, yet / Whose presence, power is / Great as no goddess's / Was deemed, dreamed who / This one work has to do / To let all God's glory through / God's glory which would go / Through her and from her flow . . .*

GERARD MANLEY HOPKINS

### JANUARY 17TH

*What ecstasy your womb knew / When all heaven's harmony / Rang out from you, For you bore the son of God / When your purity blazed on God.*

HILDEGARD OF BINGEN

### JANUARY 18TH

*I see you in a thousand paintings / Mary, so tenderly depicted / Yet none of them can begin to show you / As my soul sees you.*

NOVALIS

### JANUARY 19TH

*The power of Mary over all devils will be particularly immense in the last period of time. There will come a glorious era in which Mary will be the Ruler and Queen of human hearts.*

SAINT LOUIS-MARIE GRIGNION DE MONTFORT

### JANUARY 20TH

*The Virgin Mother is, first of all,* mater virgo—*virgin-matter or the unploughed soil—that is to say, the* Prima Materia, *prior to its division, or ploughing, into the multiplicity of created things.*

ALAN WATTS

### JANUARY 21ST

*ARY has made herself all things to all beings, and offers her merciful heart to everyone, so everyone can receive of her fullness—the slave freedom, the sick health, the afflicted consolation, the sinner pardon, and God glory; and so there can be no one anywhere who can hide from her heart.*

SAINT JEROME

JANUARY 22ND

*What a radiant flower blossomed in you / And blew fragrance to all scents / That had been barren / And all these then appeared / Brilliant in full flourish.*

HILDEGARD OF BINGEN

JANUARY 23RD

*Mary is never weary of defending us.*

SAINT GERMANUS

JANUARY 24TH

*Whatever,*

*Lady, all the Saints in union with you can obtain, you can obtain alone. . . . Why is this? Why is it that you alone have such vast power? It is because you alone are the Mother of the Redeemer of all beings; you alone are the spouse of God; you alone are the universal Queen of Heaven and Earth.*

SAINT ANSELM

JANUARY 25TH

*This is Wisdom . . . and there was given unto her hand power, honor, strength, and dominion, bearing upon her head the crown of the kingdom shining with the rays of the twelve stars, prepared as a bride adorned for her husband, and having on her garments written in golden letters in Greek, in barbarian script, and in Latin: reigning, I will reign, and my kingdom shall be without any end for all them that find me, that subtly, ingeniously, constantly, seek me out.*

THOMAS AQUINAS

JANUARY 26TH

*The Holy Mother was all beauty and all love; the sight of her overwhelmed me . . . O my Mother, most beautiful and lovable Mother, my love, heart of my heart. . . .*

MELANIE CALVAT, VISIONARY OF LA SALETTE, FRANCE, 1846

JANUARY 27TH

*When Jesus Christ sprang out of her most sacred womb, all the streams of divine gifts flowed out from Mary as if from a celestial ocean.*

SAINT BERNARDINE OF SIENNA

JANUARY 28TH

*Do not deny the Mother of the Worlds / The only thing she ever wants to see, / For it is all you ever want to find.*

HELEN SCHUEMAN

JANUARY 29TH

*If you do not reject my maternal love and practice love, my Immaculate Heart will achieve a victory in the face of the threat of a new terrifying war, and there will be love and peace in the world. . . . Have trust in me, the Mother of Peace, and rely completely on my Immaculate Heart.*

OUR LADY TO JULIA KIM, KOREA, 1991

JANUARY 30TH

*In the end, my Immaculate Heart will triumph . . . and a certain period of peace will be given to the world.*

OUR LADY, FATIMA, PORTUGAL, 1917

JANUARY 31ST

*Be thou then, O thou dear / Mother, my atmosphere.*

GERARD MANLEY HOPKINS

## A Heart Journey to Mary

*Everyone on a journey into Mary the Mother needs a handful of simple practices that work for them and that bring the Mother vividly to life in their hearts. This month I would like to suggest doing each day a very simple but powerful practice. For over a thousand years, the Orthodox tradition has used what is called the Jesus Prayer: "Lord Jesus Christ, Son of God, have mercy on me." The phrase is used as a "mantra," a sacred, empowered set of syllables or words that are repeated incessantly in the heart. The heart here is not the physical heart, but the spiritual "heart-center" that is in the center of the chest, between the breasts.*

*I find it powerful and inspiring to use what I call the Mary Prayer, said in exactly the same way, again and again, with tender fervor in the heart-center. No single "Mary mantra" has come down to us. I do not find this limiting; on the contrary, I find that this lack of definite tradition awakens personal creativity. I have evolved three Mary prayers which I use for myself depending on what I need or can feel most richly at the time: "Mary, Mother of us all, illumine me with your love," "Mary, Queen of Heaven and earth, root me in you," and sometimes just "Salve Regina" (Save, O Queen). Sometimes, also, I just repeat "Mary" quietly until the presence arrives. Everyone is a unique child of her who loves us all equally, so everyone can write for themselves their own short Mary prayer or prayers. What is essential is to practice the prayer that is yours repeatedly and with true belief.*

*How best to practice this kind of prayer? Sit comfortably, with your head slightly lowered and your eyes closed. Read the day's entry and meditate on it before doing the practice so that your mindstream is already pregnant with love of her. Then, with great concentration, slowly repeat the words of the prayer you have chosen or written, bringing to each syllable the total attention of your mind and heart.*

*Practice intensely for ten or fifteen minutes and then rest in the peace that comes. Then at moments during the day, waiting for a bus or standing in a check-out line—in fact, in any situation whatsoever—repeat the prayer for a minute or two. You will find if you do this regularly that very soon the prayer will continue of itself in your heart. You may even wake up with its syllables perfuming your mind. This kind of prayer, you will find, will instill Mary's divine presence in your heart and mindstream. Don't strain; let the words come naturally. The Mother will do the rest.*

FEBRUARY 1ST

*There is not a church without an altar in her honor, not a country, nor a canton where there are not some miraculous images, where all sorts of evil are cured and all sorts of good gifts obtained.*

SAINT LOUIS-MARIE GRIGNION DE MONTFORT

FEBRUARY 2ND *Feast of the Purification of the Virgin Mary*

*It is good to speak of her privileges, but necessary above all that we imitate her. She prefers imitation to admiration.*

SAINT THERESE OF LISIEUX

FEBRUARY 3RD

*As Eve, seduced by an Angel, turned away from God by disobedience to his word, so Mary receiving the good news from an Angel, bore God in her womb in obedience to his word; and as Eve had been led to disobey God, so Mary was persuaded to obey him. Thus the Virgin Mary became the advocate of the virgin Eve.*

SAINT IRENAEUS

FEBRUARY 4TH

FEBRUARY 4TH

*HE is our Mother. But she is also our daughter. A little girl and the Queen of Heaven. The Queen of the Angels—and yet she's still a little girl! Remember this!*

GEORGES BERNANOS

FEBRUARY 5TH

*Bright Virgin, steadfast in Eternity,*
*Star of this storm-tossed sea,*
*Trusted guide of every trustful pilot,*
*Turn your thoughts to the terrifying storm,*
*In which I find myself alone and rudderless.*

PETRARCH

FEBRUARY 6TH

*Watch over always, Lovely Lady, the needs of those devoted to you.*

BISHOP JEAN DANIELOU

## FEBRUARY 7TH

*The Roman Empire stood appalled*
*It dropped the reins of peace and war,*
*When that fierce virgin and her Star,*
*Out of the fabulous darkness called.*

WILLIAM BUTLER YEATS

## FEBRUARY 8TH

*Your breasts are as fragrant as wine; their whiteness whiter than milk and lilies;*
*their scent lovelier than flowers and balsam wood.*

ANONYMOUS, TWELFTH CENTURY

## FEBRUARY 9TH

*How sublime is this humility, which is incapable of yielding to the weight of honors,*
*or of being made proud by them! The Mother of God is chosen by God, and she de-*
*clares herself His handmaid.*

SAINT BERNARD OF CLAIRVAUX

FEBRUARY 10TH

*When you speak about her, it's always new!*

THE CURÉ OF ARS

FEBRUARY 11TH *Feast of Our Lady of Lourdes*

*The quality and the magnitude of the living star / Who surpasses there above / As she surpasses here below . . .*

DANTE

FEBRUARY 12TH

*She is the flower, the full blown rose who gives out such a scent that satisfies us all. The Mother of the Lord Most High is scented beyond any flower.*

CHARLES OF ORLEANS

FEBRUARY 13TH

*The* fiat *[yes] of Mary is Mary's consent to the divine plan of Redemption; this fiat is like the echo of the fiat of the Creation, but now what is created is a new world, a world of grace.*

DOM COLOMBA MARMION

### FEBRUARY 14TH

*She had no peer, either in our first mother or in all women who were to come. But alone of all her sex, she pleased the Lord.*

CAELIUS SEDULIUS

### FEBRUARY 15TH

*We know very well that the Blessed Virgin is Queen of Heaven and Earth, but she is more mother than queen, and she surpasses all of us in glory just as the sun at its rising makes the stars disappear. I am going to see her soon . . . soon. . . . O Blessed Virgin, O Mother, I am a baby who can't stand any more. . . . Prepare me for death.*

LAST WORDS OF SAINT THERESE OF LISIEUX

### FEBRUARY 16TH

*In Mary, the King of Heaven accomplished his spiritual nuptials with our nature. And she is the most wonderful example of exception from the common law of our nature in so many ways. No mortal, no angel, no creature ever was before or will be again the Mother of God. She is the Mother, while remaining a Virgin.*

WILLIAM ULLATHORNE

FEBRUARY 17TH

*I would be very annoyed not to go to Heaven: I wouldn't see the Virgin!*

THE CURÉ OF ARS

FEBRUARY 18TH

*Virgin of Virgins / I choose you today / As my sovereign, my queen, my empress, / And I declare myself, / Your servant and your slave.*

BARTOLOMEO DE LOS RIOS

FEBRUARY 19TH

*How I like singing for you all the time! Practicing at all moments the humblest virtues, you made visible the narrow road to Heaven.*

BLESSED ELISABETH OF THE TRINITY

FEBRUARY 20TH

*Blessed Mother, Holy Mother, in you, we all find our home!*

BLESSED GUERLIC OF IGNY

FEBRUARY 21ST

*Mary is our Mother, our sister, our brother.*
*The Savior of the World is, first of all, our brother.*
*Through Mary, our God made himself our brother.*

SAINT ANSELM

FEBRUARY 22ND

*You only need to ask her. Just ask her.*

THE CURÉ OF ARS

FEBRUARY 23RD

*As long as I draw breath, may your burning love ensure that I bear these words [Ave Maria] in my heart and in my memory.*

BARTOLOMEO DE LOS RIOS

FEBRUARY 24TH

*I see your weariness. Please, don't give up, continue in your prayers. Prayer is so vital for the world.*

OUR LADY, MEDJUGORGE, YUGOSLAVIA, 1986

*OD is our father,*
*but beyond everything, he is our mother.*

POPE JOHN PAUL I

*Mary is more blessed in receiving the faith of God than in conceiving the flesh of God.*

SAINT THOMAS AQUINAS

### FEBRUARY 27TH

*We seek refuge under the protection of your mercies, O Mother of God; do not reject our supplication, but save us from hell, O you who alone are blessed.*

ANONYMOUS, THIRD CENTURY

### FEBRUARY 28TH

*From then on, this love assaulted her so many times, her heart leapt so many times, the wound became so inflamed, that in the end, it was impossible for her not to die of it. O Passion of Love, O Love of Passion.*

SAINT FRANCIS OF SALES

### FEBRUARY 29TH

*You say, "It's raining too hard to go to church." Never speak like that! You are always praying to God to send rain to make the earth rich. Then do not turn against the blessing!*

OUR LADY, MEDJUGORGE, 1984

# March

## Ave, Ave, Ave Maria

In my daily practice of devotion to Mary, I have found this heart practice, adapted from an ancient Tibetan Buddhist meditation, not only continually helpful but transforming. It is especially powerful in times of anguish, bewilderment, and stress; the only condition necessary for its effectiveness is true sincerity.

In a cloudless bright spring sky in front of you, invoke that representation or image of Mary that has most moved your heart and with whom you feel most connected. To help you focus, place a photograph or statue of this image before you as you begin. If you cannot imagine in your heart's eye any form or picture, don't worry. Imagine Mary as the sun, or a star of tender white light.

Now, open your heart to your Mother. Be naked to all you are feeling. Keep nothing back. Know that you need feel no shame or guilt, even if the emotions that are sweeping you are dark ones. The Mother is unconditional love and knows you better than you know yourself; you have nothing to fear. Know that she is listening to *you with total attention and compassion, never for a moment judging you. Call to her now from the depths of your pain and confusion, telling her what you are going through and what you need, with the simplicity of a child addressing its mother. As you do, it helps to say a line of a prayer that truly inspires you. I often say, "Hail, Mary, full of grace" over and over again. Another friend who does this practice says the words of the ancient Russian prayer, "Mother of God, save me."*

*Imagine now that the image or representation of Mary that you have chosen begins to emit sacred white light. This light is her light, the light that is manifesting and nourishing all things in the universe. It emanates in great healing waves from whatever image you have chosen and, entering your body from the top of your head, washes it free of all psychic and physical pain. Let the light enter you and wash you fresh and clean with its immense power of love and purification, again and again, at least nine times. Each time it enters, offer up another grief, worry, or dark impulse for healing and transformation.*

*You will feel increasingly filled with the Mother's peace. As these feelings deepen, allow yourself to relax more and more; enjoy the divine smile that is growing in your heart. Finally, full of her presence, rest in her bliss, knowing yourself for all eternity her beloved child. Practice this quietly in the morning a few times, and you will find that you will be able to do it anywhere, in any circumstances, and that through it, you will feel Mary's direct love and help.*

### MARCH 1ST

*It is said that Saint Bernard used to kneel in front of each statue, each image of Our Lady, and salute it with a "Hail Mary." One day, the statue answered, "Hail Bernard."*

ANONYMOUS

### MARCH 2ND

*Mary! Feast of Glory! Feast of Motherhood! Feast of the Queen! Feast of the Empress! Feast of the Beggar! Feast of Gratitude! Feast of Joy!*

ABBE MEYNARD

### MARCH 3RD

*She is the spring of living water from which the thirsty and those who have tasted its draught bear fruit a hundred-fold.*

SAINT EPHREM

### MARCH 4TH

*I hold you in my arms. I love you. I hold you on my knees.*

OUR LADY, MEDJUGORGE, 1984

Mary! Feast of Glory! Feast of Motherhood! Feast of the Queen! Feast of the Empress! Feast of the Beggar! Feast of Gratitude! Feast of Joy! Mary! Feast of Glory! Feast of Motherhood! Feast of the Queen! Feast of the Empress! Feast of the Beggar! Feast of Gratitude! Feast of Joy! Mary! Feast of Glory! Feast of Motherhood! Feast of the Queen! Feast of the Empress! Feast of the Beggar! Feast of Gratitude! Feast of Joy! Mary! Feast of Glory! Feast of Motherhood! Feast of the Queen! Feast of the Empress! Feast of the Beggar! Feast of Gratitude! Feast of Joy! Mary! Feast of Glory! Feast of Motherhood! Feast of the Queen! Feast of the Empress! Feast of the Beggar! Feast of Gratitude! Feast of Joy! Mary! Feast of Glory! Feast of Motherhood! Feast of the Queen! Feast of the Empress! Feast of the Beggar! Feas

## MARCH 5TH

*Let Mary's soul be in each of you to glorify the Lord. Let her spirit be in each of you to rejoice in the Lord. Christ has only one mother in the flesh, but we all bring forth Christ by faith. Every soul free from the contamination of sin and inviolate in its purity can receive the word of God.*

SAINT AMBROSE

## MARCH 6TH

*The true city of the Immaculate is in your hearts.*

SAINT MAXIMILIAN KOLBE (1894-1941)

## MARCH 7TH

*Who is holier than Mary? She is unsurpassed by our ancestors, by the prophets, apostles or martyrs, by the patriarchs or the fathers, by the angels, thrones, dominions, seraphim or cherubim, or by any other created thing visible or invisible.*

ANONYMOUS, FIFTH CENTURY

MARCH 8TH

OD has a plan for each one of you. Without prayer, you will not be able to understand it.

OUR LADY, MEDJUGORGE, 1986

MARCH 9TH

*Believe what we say about the Virgin and do not hesitate to confess her to be both the servant and Mother of God, both Virgin and Mother.*

SAINT JOHN CHRYSOSTOM

MARCH 10TH

*This is the woman of history and destiny who inspires us today, the woman who speaks to us of femininity, human dignity and love, and who is the greatest expression of total consecration.*

POPE JOHN PAUL I

## MARCH 11TH

*In Heaven, the blessed thy glory proclaim,*
*On Earth we thy children invoke thy fair name,*
*Ave, Ave, Ave Maria.*
*Thy name is our power, thy virtues our light,*
*Thy love our comfort, thy pleading our might.*
*Ave, Ave, Ave Maria.*

OFFICIAL LOURDES HYMN

## MARCH 12TH

*Each time we are praising her, she praises us. If we call her a thousand times a*
*day, she will answer a thousand times.*

SAINT BERNARDINE OF SIENNA

## MARCH 13TH

*Tell everybody to ask her for what they need. Let us venerate the Immaculate*
*Heart of Mary. Tell them also to pray Mary for peace, since God has entrusted it*
*to her.*

JACINTA MARTO, CHILD OF FATIMA

MARCH 14TH

*Teach these words to all generations: Unity, Love, Faith.*

OUR LADY, SOUFANIEH, SYRIA, 1983

MARCH 15TH

*The human race could not be redeemed unless the Son of God were born of the Virgin, so the birth of the blessed and undefiled Mother of God justly brings beings a special and, indeed, unparalleled joy, for it marked the beginning of all human salvation.*

SAINT PETER DAMIAN

MARCH 16TH

*Whiter than the dawn, / Brighter than the sun, / My lovely Queen, / My sweet love.*

CHRISTIAN SONGBOOK

MARCH 17TH

*The authentic, pure feminine is, above all things, a luminous chaste energy, the vessel of the Ideal and of Goodness, the Blessed Virgin Mary.*

TEILHARD DE CHARDIN

### MARCH 18TH

*Of all the virtues of the Virgin, the most admirable is her great humility. It is a virtue of which we ourselves have a great need. We are transported when others praise us falsely. Mary was disturbed when the angel praised her truthfully, and she ended by calling herself a handmaid.*

ALFONSO DE OROZCO

### MARCH 19TH

*She is my most ancient Love. I loved her even before knowing her.*

THE CURÉ OF ARS

### MARCH 20TH

> *IRGIN of Virgins*
> *You were untouched by the stain of sin,*
> *That first of all evils,*
> *The sad inheritance of the human race;*
> *From my earliest years,*
> *I have placed my hope in you.*

LUIS DE LEON

### MARCH 21ST

*As a sign of your acceptance, / Engrave my heart with the fire of your love.*

BARTOLOMEO DE LOS RIOS

### MARCH 22ND

*In what peace and recollection did Mary live and act! The most trivial actions were sanctified by her, for through them she remained the constant adorer of the gift of God.*

BLESSED ELISABETH OF THE TRINITY

### MARCH 23RD

*Every woman who is separated from her child, every woman who must stand by helpless and see her child die, every woman who echoes the old cry, "Why my child?" has the answer from the Mother of Christ. She can look at the child through Mary's eyes, know the answer through Mary's mind, accept the suffering through Mary's will.*

FRANCES CARYLL HOUSELANDER

### MARCH 24TH

*No one has ever more perfectly contained the light of God than Mary who, by the perfection of her purity and humility is, as it were, completely identified with truth, like the clean window pane which vanishes entirely into the light which it transmits.*

THOMAS MERTON

### MARCH 25TH *Feast of the Annunciation*

*The Angel said to her, "Do not be afraid, Mary, for you have found favor, and you will conceive in your womb and bear a son, and you will name him Jesus. He will be great, and will be called the Son of the Most High, and God will give to him the throne of his ancestor David."*

LUKE 1:30-32

### MARCH 26TH

*Mary accepted with a generous heart this great and laborious function of mother, and from the time of Pentecost, we see her supporting admirably the first fruits of the Christian people with the sanctity of her examples, the authority of her counsels, the gentleness of her consolations, the efficacy of her prayers.*

POPE LEO XIII

MARCH 27TH

# Mary,
*if I were Queen of Heaven*

*and you were Therese, I would*

*pray to be Therese for you*

*to be Queen of Heaven.*

SAINT THERESE OF LISIEUX

I've asked her to follow me everywhere, and she granted me this grace. I talk to her with total trust and confidence. She may forgive our sins, but she'll never bless them.

SAINT MUTIAN-MARY OF MALONNES

## MARCH 29TH

Who ever thought that before she came the world was still unfinished?

RAINER-MARIA RILKE

## MARCH 30TH

Springtime is a long feast for Mary, our Mother. It is both the spring of the year and the spring of Nature. Mary is the spring of the world and the spring of grace. The spring is the season of flowers, and she is the flower.

ABBE MEYNARD

## MARCH 31ST

When you fall, you must not remain on the ground. You must get up. The greatest fault is to realize you have fallen and not to get up immediately.

## Mary in the Scriptures

The practice that I would like you to do this month is one that I first learned from a Hindu devotee of the Divine Mother in Benares. He told me, "Do it with any image of the Mother you want, and it will bring the same blessing." I love this practice, because it introduces anyone who does it with true passion to that wholeness of being and complete integration of body, spirit, heart, and mind that the Mother wants for each of us.

First, imagine the Mother as Mary standing above your head with her palms outspread. As always, choose that image of her that moves you most, and imagine her surrounded by white light, smiling with infinite tenderness and compassion. From her outspread palms starts to pour a stream of soft, golden light. Feel it enter you *through the top of your head. Allow this light to enter into every part of your being and body, to heal, purify, clarify, and irradiate everything in you and bring every part of you, separately and together, into a unity of peace and bliss.*

*Let the light fill your head, praying for your powers of vision and understanding to be awakened. Sometimes, you may feel a tickling between the eyebrows; this is the light starting to awaken what in mystical traditions is called the Third Eye, the spiritual eye at the center of the forehead which is opened slowly through devotion and which, in the end, sees the divine world directly. Now take the divine light down into your throat, where a center of communication is hidden. Allow the light to open that center as sunlight opens a shy red rose.*

*Now, with your head and throat gently on fire, take the light down into the heart center. The heart center is the core and guide of your divine human being; awakening its boundless love and all-embracing sky-like compassion—which are one with her love and compassion—is the most important aspect of the journey into her. Rest, now, in your light-opened heart, and feel how her light in you aligns head and heart, mind and psyche, intellect and emotion.*

*Established now in her divine love, take the light down, first into your belly, allowing it to become "pregnant" with the light's full sweetness, and then, without any shame whatsoever, down into your genital area. A great deal of human pain comes from sexual wounding, from the wounds that millennia of body-hatred have inflicted on all of us. Mary wants all of our instincts to be consecrated to her and brought to their full rich life in her. One of her aspects is holy Eros, and one of the greatest freedoms that she wants to give humanity is that of a sanctified sexuality. So allow her light to enter the sexual area and heal all of the fears, repressions, and remembered humiliations that are stored there.*

*Now, take the light even further down—down the thighs, down the kneecaps, down the back of the legs, and down the ankles to the ends of the toes. As you do so, also extend the light along your shoulders and arms to the end of your fingers. When the practice is complete, you will feel your whole body and being alight with her— every part of you, head, heart, body, and soul, in radiant harmony.*

*At the end of the practice, pray to Mary for the grace of experiencing this harmony ever more completely and for the insight and the courage to integrate it at ever deeper levels into all aspects of your life.*

APRIL 1ST

*I will make you a great nation, I will bless you and make your name great, and you will be a blessing.*

GENESIS 12:2

APRIL 2ND

EAR, O daughter, consider and incline your ear; forget your people and your father's house, and the king will desire your beauty. Since he is your Lord, bow to him.

PSALMS 45:10–11

APRIL 3RD

*With me are riches, glorious riches. . . . That I may enrich them who love me.*

PROVERBS 8:18–21

### APRIL 4TH

*For thus says the Lord: I will extend prosperity to her like a sea, and the wealth of the Nations like an overflowing stream; and you shall nurse, and be carried on her arms, and dandled on her knees. As a mother comforts her child, so I will comfort you, and you shall be comforted in Jerusalem.*

ISAIAH 66:12–13

### APRIL 5TH

*For she is an infinite treasure to human beings, and they that use her become the friends of God.*

WISDOM 7:14

### APRIL 6TH

*Set me as a seal upon your heart, as a seal upon your arm; for love is strong as death, passion fierce as the grave. Its flashes are flashes of fire, a raging fire.*

SONG OF SONGS 8:6

APRIL 7TH

*O Lord, my heart is not lifted up, my eyes are not raised too high; I do not occupy myself with things too great and too marvelous for me. I have calmed and quieted my soul like a weaned child with his mother; my soul is like the weaned child that is with me.*

PSALMS 131:1–2

APRIL 8TH

*And the Angel of the Lord said to the woman: "You shall conceive and bear a son. No razor is to come on his head, for the boy shall be a Nazirite to God from birth. He is the one who shall begin to deliver Israel from the hand of the Philistines."*

JUDGES 13:3–5

APRIL 9TH

*Mary said to the Angel: "How is this to take place, since I am a virgin?" The Angel answered: "The Holy Spirit will come upon you and the power of the most high will overshadow you; therefore the child to be born will be holy; he will be called Son of God."*

LUKE 1:34–35

APRIL 10TH

*One is my dove: My perfect one is but one.*

SONG OF SONGS 6:8

APRIL 11TH

HEREFORE the Lord

*himself will* ... *give you a sign. Look,* ... *the young woman is with child, and* ... *shall bear a son, and* ... *shall name him Immanuel.*

ISAIAH 7:14

APRIL 12TH

*And Mary said: "Here Am I,* ... *the servant of the Lord; let it be with me, according to your word."*

LUKE 1:38

APRIL 13TH

*Before she was in labor, she gave birth. Before her pain came upon her, she delivered a son. Who has heard of such a thing? Who has seen such things? Shall a land be born in one day? Shall a nation be delivered in one moment? Yet as soon as Zion was in labor, she delivered her children.*

ISAIAH 66:7-8

APRIL 14TH

*In the Canticles it is written: "My sister, my spouse, is a garden enclosed." Our Lord planted in this holy and sublime garden, this sacred paradise of tenderness, all the flowers which would adorn his church. . . . Amongst a hundred others, the violet of humility, the lily of purity, and the full red rose of charity.*

SAINT BERNARD OF CLAIRVAUX

APRIL 15TH

*Your neck is like an ivory tower; your eyes are pools in Heshbon by the gate of Bath-Rabbim. Your nose is like a tower of Lebanon, overlooking Damascus. How fair and pleasant you are, O Loved One, delectable maiden.*

SONG OF SONGS 7:4-6

APRIL 16TH

*While he was saying this, a woman in the crowd raised her voice and said to him: "Blessed is the womb that bore you and the breasts that nursed you."*

LUKE 1:27–28

APRIL 17TH

*And Mary said: "My soul magnifies the Lord and my spirit rejoices in God, for he has looked with favor on the lowliness of his servant."*

LUKE 1:47–48

APRIL 18TH

*Noah's ark was a type for Mary: For just as through the ark men were preserved from the flood, so, by Mary, we are all saved from the shipwreck of sin, but with this difference: only a few were saved in the ark. Through Mary, the whole human race was saved from death.*

SAINT BERNARD

APRIL 19TH

*She is the Rose of Sharon, the lily of the valley, the dove in the clefts of the rocks, the pillar of marble, the dawn, the moon, the sun.*

SAINT BERNARD, COMMENTARY TO THE SONG OF SONGS

APRIL 20TH

*And why has this happened to me, that the mother of my Lord comes to me? For as soon as I heard the sound of your greeting, the child in my womb leaped for joy.*

LUKE 1:43-44

APRIL 21ST

*Mother: "They have no wine." Jesus: "What have I to do with you? My hour is not yet come." Mother: [To the crowd] "Whatsoever he saith unto you, do it."*

JOHN 2:3-5

APRIL 22ND

*Listen to me, O coast lands; pay attention, you people far away! The Lord called me before I was born; while I was in my mother's womb, he named me.*

ISAIAH 49:1

APRIL 23RD

*And blessed is she who believed that there would be a fulfillment of what was spoken to her by the Lord.*

LUKE 1:45

APRIL 24TH

*And she gave birth to a son, a male child, who is to rule all the nations with a rod of iron. But her child was snatched away and taken to God and to his throne; and the woman fled into the wilderness where she has a place prepared by the Lord.*

REVELATION 12:5–6

APRIL 25TH

*Surely from now on all generations will call me blessed.*

LUKE 1:48

APRIL 26TH

*Hannah made this vow: "O Lord of Hosts, if only you will look on the misery of your servant and remember me, and not forget your servant, but will give to your servant a male child, then, I will set him before you as a Nazirite until the day of his death."*

SAMUEL 1:11

APRIL 27TH

*Blessed is she who trusted, who believed.*

LUKE 1:45

APRIL 28TH

*After three days, they found him in the temple . . . and his mother said to him: "Son, why have you done this to us? You see that your father and I have been searching for you in sorrow."*

LUKE 2:48

APRIL 29TH

*Listen! I am waiting at the door, knocking; if your hear my voice and open the door, I will come in to you and eat with you, and you with me.*

REVELATION 3:20

APRIL 30TH

*Then he went down with them and came to Nazareth and was obedient to them. His mother treasured all these things in her heart.*

LUKE 2:51

---------------------------------------

*For over a hundred and fifty years, the Mother as Mary has been appearing all over the world, usually to children or very young people, sending through them to the whole of humanity simple, essential messages and warnings. What she is saying is clear: unless the whole human race turns to love and invites love to inform all its actions and choices, the world will be plunged into terminal chaos. We are, she reminds us again and again, at a crucial moment of history; unless we transform ourselves, we will die out, and take Nature with us in a deathdance of unimaginable horror and agony.*

*Alongside these unambiguous and anguished warnings, Mary is also—as one would expect of the Divine Mother who is all love and protection—giving the whole of humanity the certainty of her endless encouragement and support, and opening out to the entire human race a simple way of always being in touch with her and receptive to her transforming power. Again and again she tells us to pray simply, to share what we have, to believe in the reality and goodness of God, to do everything in our power to feed the poor and reverse the policies of exploitation that are ruining our earth. Even at this potentially final moment, the Mother is offering the way out of disaster, the way of her simplicity, her love, her unending and humble commitment to put love into action in every arena of life.*

*Traditionally, May is dedicated to Mary. I have devoted the month to her messages to us. A great Spring is being prepared for humankind, but we can share in it only if we are prepared to follow the way of the Mother. Each of Mary's messages gives us another vital clue as to what this way consists in and demands. I invite you every day to read the message of the day and then examine what in you prevents you from understanding or enacting what Mary is trying to ask us to do. Then, using one of the meditations that has already been given, offer up whatever resistances to her simplicity that you find in yourself for her healing and transformation.*

*"I am the Queen of Peace," Mary has announced again and again. Let each of us, every day, offer up our whole being to her to be made into instruments of that Great Peace that she wills for the whole creation.*

## MAY 1ST

*My children, if you want to be very happy in this life, lead a simple life, pray a great deal, and do not delve into your problems, but let the Divine solve them.*

OUR LADY, MEDJUGORGE, 1981

## MAY 2ND

*I am the Mother of the poor.*
*I came here to heal the pain of the world.*

OUR LADY, BANNEUX, BELGIUM, FEBRUARY, 1933

## MAY 3RD

*I beg you, destroy the house made of cardboard which you have built on dirty desires. Then I will be able to act for you .*

OUR LADY, MEDJUGORGE, 1986

## MAY 4TH

*What I do in you is always up to you.*

OUR LADY, MEDJUGORGE, 1983

MAY 5TH

If God can clothe in such splendor the grass
of the fields, will he not provide
much more for you, O weak
in faith!

OUR LADY, MEDJUGORGE, 1984

MAY 6TH

OU can always find me
in the less fortunate.

OUR LADY, BANNEUX, 1933

MAY 7TH

*What did you see?*
*Something white.*
*Something or somebody?*
*I don't know. . . . It looked like a pretty young girl.*

INTERROGATION OF BERNADETTE
SOUBIROUS, LOURDES, FRANCE, 1858

MAY 8TH

*Help one another, and I will help you.*

OUR LADY, MEDJUGORGE, 1983

MAY 9TH

*To all those who recite my rosary devoutly, I promise my special protection and many great graces.*

OUR LADY, BEAURAING, BELGIUM, 1932

MAY 10TH

*Love is the simplest, most beautiful, and purest form of prayer.*

OUR LADY, SCOTTSDALE, 1988

MAY 11TH

*I do not need a hundred Our Fathers or Hail Marys! It is much better to pray one with real desire to encounter God.*

OUR LADY, MEDJUGORGE, 1985

MAY 12TH

*Love one another. Forgive each other. Make peace. It is not enough to ask for peace; make peace! Do not turn to violence. Never have recourse to violence.*

OUR LADY, CUAPA, NICARAGUA, 1980

MAY 13TH

*All my children think I am far away, but I am always right beside you. I never leave you. Never! Not even for a moment. If you open your hearts, you will be able to recognize me. And you will know how much I love you.*

OUR LADY, MEDJUGORGE, FIRST APPARITION, 1981

MAY 14TH

*Believe in me; I will believe in you.*

LAST WORDS OF OUR LADY, BANNEUX, 1933

## MAY 15TH

*My coming is a sign to all of you and a call to pray and live the days of grace that God is giving you. Therefore, dear children, accept the call to prayer with seriousness. I am with you, and your suffering is also mine.*

OUR LADY, MEDJUGORGE, 1982

## MAY 16TH

*You will experience happiness by loving one another. Love is a deep passion which flows with purity. Allow your love to be shared by passing it on through your actions. Return to basic principles of loving and respecting one another.*

OUR LADY, SCOTTSDALE, 1988

## MAY 17TH

*Do not look with scorn on the poor man who is begging a morsel of bread from your abundant table. Help him, and I will help you.*

OUR LADY, MEDJUGORGE, 1986

MAY 18TH

*I, your Holy Mother, have come back to ask for peace. The world is in a terrible state. Pray for peace. Act for peace. Feed the poor. It is for this reason that I speak in many places over the entire world.*

OUR LADY, TERRA BIANCA, MEXICO, 1987

MAY 19TH

*Pray, pray, pray with all your strength. In prayer is the solution for every situation.*

OUR LADY, FATIMA, 1917

MAY 20TH

*Without love, you will achieve nothing.*

OUR LADY, MEDJUGORGE, 1984

MAY 21ST

*I am the Mother of God, / I am the Queen of Heaven, / Pray always.*

LAST WORDS OF OUR LADY, BEAURAING, 1933

### MAY 22ND

*I know you are tired. But your mother is tireless and wishes to comfort you.*

OUR LADY, SCOTTSDALE, 1988

### MAY 23RD

*If you follow me, you will discover God in everything, even in the smallest flower. You will discover a great joy!*

OUR LADY, MEDJUGORGE, 1989

### MAY 24TH

*My children, pray, so that in the whole world the Kingdom of Love can come. How happy humankind will be then!*

OUR LADY, FATIMA, 1917

### MAY 25TH

*Why don't you respond to my supplication? Talk with other people, find solutions for the world! Don't wait for the next war!*

OUR LADY, SAN DAMIANO, 1967

MAY 26TH

*If you abandon yourselves to me, you will not even feel the passage from this life to the next life. You will begin to live the life of heaven on earth.*

OUR LADY, MEDJUGORGE, 1986

MAY 27TH

*Do not listen to anyone! Do not listen to these new theories! You must love and pray and help. This is the only solution.*

OUR LADY, SAN DAMIANO, 1967

MAY 28TH

*You think that I am beautiful? I am beautiful because I love. Do not imagine that your mother is more blessed than you. All who live in Love are blessed as I.*

OUR LADY, SAN DAMIANO, 1966

MAY 29TH

*You must work in the world. God did not create wars. God did not create weapons. I will give you all my help, but it is your responsibility, your duty to act for a better world.*

OUR LADY TO ROSA QUATTRINI, SAN DAMIANO, 1968

MAY 30TH

*You have the choice every day to open your hearts or not.*

LEASE,

*put into action all my words, the words of your mother!*

*Heal my wounded heart by your love for one other!*

OUR LADY, SAN DAMIANO, 1967

MAY 31ST *Feast of Our Lady of All Graces*

*These are the times of the great return. Yes, after the time of the great suffering, there will be the time of the great rebirth, and all will blossom again. Humanity will again be a new garden of life and of beauty.*

OUR LADY, MEDJUGORGE, 1986

# June

## Mother of Love

*Really to hear what Mary has been saying to us in her messages all through May is, inevitably, to risk awakening primal forms of fear and anxiety. After all, Mary is making clear to us that the world is in terrible danger and that everything we love or cherish is menaced, unless a massive spiritual and political transformation takes place, very fast.*

*What I want to offer for the month of June is a meditation that I have found invaluable in transforming fear and anxiety of all kinds into peace of mind and a strong, humble resolve. Part of this meditation derives from an ancient Taoist visualization; the other part I have gradually evolved myself.*

*Imagine before you a vast, black, boiling darkness. In this blackness boils all* the evil, greed, and chaos of nature and the world. The darkness is all-encompassing, sweeps from horizon to horizon, and is so powerful that a part of you feels that at any moment it could annihilate you.

Allow the full force of this terrible darkness to strike. Then hear a quiet voice from within you say, "Every fear or anxiety you fling into the darkness with real trust and joy will turn into a star." Encouraged, seize every fear or anxiety as it arises and fling it with your full force into the boiling darkness before you. The moment after you have done so, imagine that a star explodes open before you. Continue flinging all the different dark thoughts that arise in you into the darkness. If you go on flinging them with trust and passion into the darkness, you will see that the different exploding stars will coalesce and come together in a rapturous flowing movement to create in front of your eyes exactly that image of Mary that is most sacred to you. A great secret becomes clear; you begin to realize that it is your courage and trust that awaken in your inmost being that image of Mary, of the Divine Mother, that is your deepest identity. Slowly, wonderfully, Mary the Mother appears before you in the sky, created out of your own powers of trust, your own longing to be freed from fear so as to enter and enact your deepest nature, and the divine courage natural to it.

Mary in splendor stands before you, alive in light. Now, allow the bliss streaming from her eyes, the fire of the light streaming from all her limbs and every *fold of her dress, to sweep your whole being, again and again, removing as it does so every terror and every anxiety. As you are filled more and more completely with her peace and force, the darkness in front of you also starts to drain away. As you begin to burn in love and to resolve more and more strongly, the light grows more and more powerful and the darkness disappears.*

*At last, there is nothing but you and the sweetly burning diamond light of the Mother united beyond thought and stretching from one side of the horizon to the other. Rest in that peace and the courage it emanates. Rest in your identity with her. After you have finished the meditation, pray to Mary to remove all fear and panic from the heart of all beings. Now, one with her, pray: "Mother, free all beings from fear; Mother, awaken your courage in each heart; Mother, unite us all in a humble passion to serve all beings and protect and preserve your world."*

JUNE 1ST

*Through the Holy Virgin, all things are recalled to, and reinstated in, their original pristine perfection.*

SAINT ANSELM

JUNE 2ND

*The Angels offer thee a hymn; the heavens, a star / The Magi, gifts; the shepherds, their wonder / The earth, its cave; the wilderness, a manger / And we offer thee a Virgin Mother.*

CHRISTIAN HYMN

JUNE 3RD

*O face of radiant love / You have never deceived me.*

SOLOVIEV

JUNE 4TH

*The heart of Mary was the spring where Jesus fetched the blood with which he redeemed us.*

THE CURÉ OF ARS

JUNE 5TH

*She is just asking us all to be simple.*

IVAN, CHILD OF MEDJUGORGE

JUNE 6TH

*ESUS is entirely in Mary, and Mary entirely in Jesus; or rather she is no longer "herself"; you could separate light from the sun more easily than Mary from Jesus. So that you could call our Lord, Jesus of Mary, and the Holy Virgin, Mary of Jesus.*

SAINT LOUIS-MARIE GRIGNION DE MONTFORT

JUNE 7TH

*If we really knew who she is, we would die instantly of happiness.*

THE CURÉ OF ARS

JUNE 8TH

*My true mother gave me life.*

GOSPEL OF THOMAS, 55

JUNE 9TH

*Tell us, what fire burned in you, what flames leapt up, as the furnace that is God descended into your tender womb and his abyss of sweetness thrust itself into your stomach?*

SAINT THOMAS OF VILLANOVA

JUNE 10TH

*Dear children, I wish to tell you: Always pray before your work and end your work with prayer. If you do that, you and your work will be blessed. In prayer, you will find rest.*

OUR LADY, MEDJUGORGE, 1984

JUNE 11TH

*In Mary, we find the purest essence of womanhood, so concentrated that the light of the ideal flows down from her to invest every woman with something of its splendor.*

o · FATHER JAMES

JUNE 12TH

*I am the Mother of everything created by God, the "woman clothed with the sun," the new Eve who will lead mankind to light, the one who will make it possible for beings to attain eternity.*

OUR LADY TO GLADYS QUIROGA, ECUADOR, 1988

JUNE 13TH

*The Mother comes preceded by an almost blinding light, like a flashbulb. She usually wears a long gray dress, a white veil, and a beautiful crown made of twelve stars. Her eyes are blue, her hair black, and her cheeks rosy. She floats on a shining cloud that never touches the ground.*

VICKA, VISIONARY OF MEDJUGORGE

JUNE 14TH

*What does it matter if they do not believe me! I know she is there! She trusts men. She wants happiness on earth. She will convert the sinners. They can kill me if they want. I know what I see: the Blessed Mother.*

ROSA QUATTRINI, SAN DAMIANO

### JUNE 15TH

*Now here is a very strange paradox. All wells hold still water; only in the Bride is
there said to be running water. She has the depth of a well together with the constant
flow of a river.*

GREGORY OF NYSSA

### JUNE 16TH

*O flower, you did not blossom from dew
Or from drops of rain
The air did not fly around you
Divine clarity engendered you
On its noblest stem.*

HILDEGARD OF BINGEN

### JUNE 17TH

*Who has ever been stronger than Mary? / Anyone then who wishes to live in the valley
Of humility must conquer / All the power of great love.*

HADEWIJCH OF ANTWERP

JUNE 18TH

*Open to us, O Mary, the gates of Paradise, since you have the keys.*

SAINT AMBROSE

JUNE 19TH

*She bore a human body, yet she observed the kind of life that Angels live and she was a compact mountain, a rich mountain. A compact mountain, compact of body and soul; a rich mountain, rich in divine grace, by which she is proclaimed complete.*

JOHN WALDEBY

JUNE 20TH

*Your loving kindness helps not only him*
*Who asks, but time and time again*
*Freely it anticipates the asking.*

*In you is mercy, is sublime pity,*
*In you magnificence of heart, in you is joined*
*Every goodness that is in every creature.*

DANTE

### JUNE 21ST

*Little ones, the Creator has created you so wonderfully! Pray that life may be full of joy and thanksgiving and that they may flow out of your heart like a river of joy. My little children, give thanks unceasingly for all that you possess and will receive.*

OUR LADY, MEDJUGORGE, 1988

### JUNE 22ND

*The titles of Mary are many, and it is right that I should use them, for she is the palace where dwells forever the omnipotent King of Kings.*

SAINT EPHREM

### JUNE 23RD

*Although others before her strove for love, / Men could best understand it through her. / She observed the law and family traditions, / But paid no heed to rewards, threats, praise, or laments. / So she left all for the sake of her unique Beloved. / Justly then did Love exalt her, / When Love made her the Mother of Love.*

HADEWIJCH OF ANTWERP

JUNE 24TH

*And Elizabeth calls her who was yet a virgin, Mother, prophetically by her word anticipating the event, and names the Savior the fruit of her womb, because he was not to be from man, but from the Mother alone.*

ORIGEN

JUNE 25TH

*Rejoice, for you are full of grace, says the Angel. Yes, full! For while a share of grace was granted to others, the undiminished fullness of grace was poured into Mary.*

SAINT
PASCHASSIUS
RADBERT

JUNE 26TH

*Turn off the television; put aside all useless things. I invite you to turn over your hearts to me.*

OUR LADY, MEDJUGORGE, 1986

JUNE 27TH

*Let my sacred heart become yours.*
*Live and act from my love.*
*Risk everything while there is still time.*
*Give everything while there is still time.*

ANDREW HARVEY

JUNE 28TH

*Live peace in your heart and in your surroundings, so that all recognize peace, which does not come from you, but from God.*

OUR LADY, MEDJUGORGE, 1988

JUNE 29TH

*Though the enemy and devil seduced Eve, and Adam fell with her, yet the Lord not only granted them a Redeemer but also granted us all in the woman, the ever-virgin Mary, who crushes the head of the serpent in herself and in all the human race, an invincible intercessor who cannot be put to shame. That is why the Mother of God is called the "wounding of demons." It is not possible for demons to destroy a man so long as he has recourse to the help of the Mother.*

SAINT SERAPHIM OF SAROV

JUNE 30TH

*I want you to be happy now. This time is for you.*

OUR LADY, MEDJUGORGE, 1988

# July

## Let the Whole Earth Praise Her

Mary our Mother is always with us, closer to us than our own jugular vein, more intimately interwoven with our being than our own breath, always holding us in infinite love to her heart, always trying to inspire us into our deepest, calmest, and finest selves. Waking up to the miracle of this all-enfolding passionate concern from the Mother of the Universe is the most wonderful thing that can happen to anyone in this life and the entry into the conscious human divine childhood that awaits all true lovers of the Mother.

Our tragedy is that we are so rarely open to the one who is always open to us, so rarely vulnerable to the one whose always-open heart is so vulnerable to our pain and difficulties, so rarely awake to the messages that are always arising out of her silence. This is why learning to "inspire" ourselves is so important. A Christian saint,

Bede Griffiths, once said to me, "What is essential is to keep the heart always open to beauty, for she is beauty." What could be harder in an age like ours? And yet, it is just because our age is so harsh and brutal that it is more than ever essential to create around us, in our homes and offices and meeting places, a sacred environment. To do so is to awaken the poet in each of us, the poet and the lover of life and beauty.

Creating a sacred environment is not complicated; it just requires concentration and the constant reminder that the one important thing in your life is to keep your heart open to Divine Love. I find that having a small altar to the Mother in every room of the house helps; listening to great sacred music provides constant joy; reading one or two lines of an inspiring sacred text or a poem to her before beginning my day ensures that it begins subtly perfumed by her. Finding time to walk in the park or by the sea brings her close.

When I do these simple practices, I find that I talk to her more during the course of my day; I find myself asking her advice about all sorts of things—relationships, business arrangements, even what kinds of fruits and vegetables to buy, inviting her inwardly to meetings with friends and colleagues. The Mother is far simpler than we are; she does not need fancy invocations or elaborate images. Just like a human mother, she is delighted by anything one of her children offers her in love; a pebble or a daffodil enchant her just as much—or more—than a jewel or a gold statue. All that matters to her is our sincerity. One stick of incense lit to her in true adoration delights her as much as a thousand masses.

This month I invite you to transform your environment into one sacred to her. Meditate on what brings you simply into her presence and see that you regularly find time to do it. Make your homes temples to her, by putting up small altars, playing sacred music in her honor, inviting her into every activity from cooking to vacuuming to walking to the shops to answering dull letters. Very soon the rewards of such remembrance will start arriving—in deeper inner stability and a constant subtle sense of joy running like a stream under all other thoughts and work. Ordinary life, if she is constantly involved in it, will slowly reveal her face in all of its details and become what it essentially is—the normal flow of her unbroken miracle.

## JULY 1ST

*Why are you so sunk in thought? The Woman in the Sun*
*Who stands upon the Moon, must first become your soul.*

ANGELUS SILESIUS

## JULY 2ND *Feast of the Visitation*

*O greening branch / You stand in your nobility / Like*
*the rising dawn. / Rejoice now and exult / And deign*
*to free the fools we are / From our long slavery to evil /*
*And hold out your hand / To raise us up.*

HILDEGARD OF BINGEN

## JULY 3RD

*Hail field that flourishes with the fertility of compassion! / Hail table that bears a*
*wealth of mercy! / Hail to you who makes meadows of delight blossom! / Hail to you*
*who draws out of the depths of darkness / The diamond of eternal passion and eter-*
*nal love!*

ROMANUS MELODOS, AKATHIST HYMN TO THE
VIRGIN, BYZANTIUM, FIFTH CENTURY

### JULY 4TH

*When he named her, he wanted his heart to leave his chest: He declared that this sweetest of names was like a honeycomb melting in the inmost depth of his soul.*

HENRY SUSO

### JULY 5TH

*The threefold terror of love; a fallen flare*
*Through the hollow of an ear;*
*Wings beating about the room;*
*The terror of all terrors that I bore*
*The heavens in my womb.*

WILLIAM BUTLER YEATS

### JULY 6TH

*Mary has arrived at that fullness of the God-like life of grace which for the rest of the creation remains to be revealed.*

SERGEI BULGAKOV

### JULY 7TH

*Holy Mother of God, save us.*

OLD RUSSIAN PRAYER

### JULY 8TH

*O you who are full of grace, you who are the joy of every creature, of the host of Angels and the race of men.*

ORTHODOX LITURGY

### JULY 9TH

*Mary is created Wisdom, for she is creation glorified. In her, creation is utterly irradiated by its archetype. God, in her, is already all in all.*

SERGEI BULGAKOV

### JULY 10TH

*He who finds Mary finds every good.*

RAYMOND JORDANO

### JULY 11TH

*Let not my titles, crowns, and worldly honors / Cause me to glory in my rank and beauty. / Emperors are thy servants as are kings. / I am a Queen myself—and your handmaiden.*

MARIE DE MEDICIS, QUEEN OF FRANCE

### JULY 12TH

*The treasure at the heart of the rose*
*Is your own heart's treasure,*
*Scatter it as the rose does:*
*Your pain becomes hers to measure.*

GABRIELA MISTRAL

### JULY 13TH

*Sophia! You of the whirling wings, / Circling encompassing energy of God: / You quicken the world in your clasp. / One wing soars in heaven; one wing sweeps the earth, / And the third flies all around us. / All praise to Sophia! Let the whole earth praise her!*

HILDEGARD OF BINGEN

## JULY 14TH

*The greatest sin is to rebel against the Motherhood of God and to refuse to recognize me as the Mother of all human beings.*

OUR LADY, FATIMA, 1917

## JULY 15TH

*For I am the first, and the last.*
*I am the honored one and the scorned.*
*I am the whore and the holy one.*
*I am the wife and the virgin.*
*I am the mother and the daughter.*
*And every part of both.*

THE THUNDER: PERFECT MIND, GNOSTIC GOSPEL

## JULY 16TH *Feast of Our Lady of Mount Carmel*

*O no man knows through what wild centuries roves back the rose.*

WALTER DE LA MARE

JULY 17TH

*In the Resurrection and Assumption of Our Lady, the creation of the world may be said to have been brought to completion and its end achieved: "Wisdom is justified of her children" [Matthew 11:19]. In her the world has already become glorious, divine, and worthy of the regard of God.*

SERGEI BULGAKOV

JULY 18TH

*The Virgin is a crystal, her Son divine light:*
*She is utterly pierced by him, but stays untouched.*

ANGELUS SILESIUS

JULY 19TH

*Mary is the hidden force and secret of Christianity, and until her force—the force of the Divine Mother—is revealed and uncovered in the Christian story, its whole truth cannot be present.*

ANDREW HARVEY

JULY 20TH

*In relation to the Father, she is named daughter; in relation to the Son, mother and bride, unwedded bride of God; in relation to the Spirit, she is the spirit bearer, the Glory of the World.*

SERGEI BULGAKOV

JULY 21ST

*It is through the very holy Virgin that Jesus Christ came into the world to begin with, and it is also through her that he will reign in the world.*

SAINT LOUIS-MARIE GRIGNION DE MONTFORT

JULY 22ND

*Hail, QUEEN Wisdom, may the Lord keep you safe, with your sister, Holy Pure Simplicity.*

SAINT FRANCIS OF ASSISI

JULY 23RD

*Whoever does not listen to my Lady / Will be eternally deaf to happiness / And never again hear or see / The highest melody and wonder of powerful love. / Whoever flies and goes the ways my Lady loves / Shall be powerful in the kingdom of love.*

HADEWIJCH OF ANTWERP

JULY 24TH

*Know that God becomes a child, lies in the womb of the Virgin*
*So I can grow like him, and gather to me Godhead.*

ANGELUS SILESIUS

JULY 25TH

*For I am knowledge and ignorance.*
*I am modesty and boldness,*
*I am shameless, I am ashamed,*
*I am strength and I am fear.*
*I am war and I am peace.*

THE THUNDER: PERFECT MIND, GNOSTIC GOSPEL

### JULY 26TH

*The Virgin births the son of God externally,*
*I do it in spirit, God the Father in Eternity.*

ANGELUS SILESIUS

### JULY 27TH

*Through Mary, God prepared the world for the first coming of Christ.*
*Through Mary, he is preparing the world now for a second coming.*

OUR LADY, MEDJUGORGE

### JULY 28TH

*Not everything is close to God; the Virgin and the Child.*
*These two, and these only, shall be God's play-mates.*

ANGELUS SILESIUS

### JULY 29TH

*Eternal Wisdom builds; May I become her palace!*
*For she has found in me—and I in her—all peace.*

ANGELUS SILESIUS

JULY 30TH

*Mary is, in personal form, the human likeness of the Holy Ghost. Through her, with her human form become entirely transparent to the Holy Ghost, we have a manifestation and, as it were, a personal revelation of him.*

SERGEI BULGAKOV

JULY 31ST

*say that we are wound*
*With mercy round and round*
*As if with air: the same*
*Is Mary, more by name.*
*She, wild web, wondrous robe,*
*Mantles the guilty globe,*
*Since God has let dispense*
*Her prayers his providence:*
*Nay, more than almoner,*
*The sweet alm's self is her*
*And men are meant to share*
*Her life as life does air.*

GERARD MANLEY HOPKINS

# Prayers

On August 15th occurs what for many lovers of Mary is her supreme Feast Day—the Assumption, which celebrates Mary's being taken up into heaven "body and soul." The Assumption was declared official dogma by the Catholic Church in 1950.

As Carl Jung was the first to recognize, the declaration of the dogma of the Assumption marked a significant turning point in the relationship of the Western imagination to the Sacred Feminine. As Jung pointed out, the dogma enshrines officially the sanctification of matter, the declaration that the entire universe, through Mary's being lifted body and soul into heaven, is now utterly sacred. What the Assumption celebrates, in fact, is nothing less than the redemption of matter, of all the matter of the universe, and its ultimate consecration in the Godhead. Jung believed passionately that this blessing of the Creation opened up to us all a new way of loving reality, a great opportunity to heal the false

# ugust

divisions and separations between body and soul, earth and heaven, prayer and action that have plagued the human religious imagination, and especially "official" Christianity, with its emphasis on original sin and its sometimes only barely disguised misogyny, body hatred, and denigration of the natural world.

The dogma of the Assumption also helps us all understand more clearly Mary's enormous role in the Christian revelation. Just as Mary shared the agony of her Son's crucifixion, so she shared in the glory of his resurrection. Christ's reappearance in a Light-Body after his victory over death signaled the beginning of a New Creation, in which everything is saturated with the divine energy of rebirth. Mary remained on earth to extend and deepen the Light-Path her Son had opened up.

For the twenty or so years Mary remained on earth after Jesus' ascension, she was, I believe, engaged in a massive silent work of integrating the New Light with matter, first in her own being and then, by extension, in the whole matter of

creation. Mary united in her own being and body heaven and earth, matter and spirit, and so earned the human and divine right to take her own body, uncorrupted by death, directly into the divine. With it, by radiant implication, she took the whole of the informed and transformed matter of the universe, a universe whose subtle laws had forever been altered by the miracle of the resurrection of her Son and by the lonely and magnificent courage of her own Light-Work—of her calling down the Light into this dimension and this world, into its every nook and cranny, down even into the most recalcitrant cells of the body.

The terms of life-in-creation were entirely transformed by Christ and Mary working together in an astounding "double" alchemy; this divine alchemical dance of Mother and Son is, for me, the mystical secret of Christianity. Keeping the mystical meaning of the Assumption always in your mind and heart, say the prayers of this month to her who, through her humility and heart wisdom, glorified the entire creation.

## AUGUST 1ST

*Remember, O most gracious Virgin, / that never was it known / that anyone who fled to thy protection, / implored thy help, / or sought thy intercession / was left unaided. / Inspired with this confidence, / I fly to thee, O Virgin of Virgins, my mother. / To thee do I come, before thee I stand, / sinful and sorrowful. / O Mother of the Word Incarnate, / despise not my petitions, / but in mercy, hear and answer me. Amen.*

THE MEMORARE

## AUGUST 2ND

*Holy Virgin of Virgins,*
*Mother of good counsel,*
*Virgin most wise,*
*Mother most pure,*
*Virgin most faithful,*
*Pray for us.*

LITANY OF LORETO, ITALY

*Now, as we recall the apparitions of Mary, may we be granted increased health of mind and body, through the same Jesus Christ, Mary's son, who lives and reigns with you and the Holy Spirit, one God, world without end. Amen.*

PRAYER TO OUR LADY OF LOURDES

*Show thyself a Mother,*
*May the ㅤㅤㅤㅤㅤㅤ ORD divine*
*Born for us your infant,*
*Hear our prayers through thine.*

AVE MARIS STELLA (HAIL O STAR OF OCEAN), NINTH CENTURY

## AUGUST 5TH

*Glorious Virgin, joy to you,*
*Loveliest whom in Heaven they view,*
*Fairest where all are fair,*
*Plead with Christ our sins to spare.*

AVE REGINA COELORUM (HAIL, O QUEEN
OF HEAVEN), TWELFTH CENTURY

## AUGUST 6TH

*Rejoice, key of the kingdom of Christ!*
*Rejoice, impregnable wall of the kingdom!*
*Rejoice, thou through whom we obtain our victories!*
*Rejoice, healing of my body!*
*Rejoice, salvation of my soul!*

ROMANUS MELODOS,
AKATHIST HYMN TO THE VIRGIN

AUGUST 7TH

*To you, Beloved Mother, and to your Immaculate Heart, we give and consecrate ourselves. May our sacrifices and recitations of the Rosary win the grace of conversion for many souls and so hasten the triumph of the Kingdom of your Son, our Lord Jesus Christ, in whose name we pray. Amen.*

PRAYER TO OUR LADY OF FATIMA, 1917

AUGUST 8TH

*O Sweet Mother! Fount of Love,*
*Touch my spirit from above,*
*Make my heart with yours accord,*
*Make me feel as you have felt*
*Make my soul to glow and melt.*

STABAT MATER, ATTRIBUTED TO
JACOPONE DA TODI, FOURTEENTH CENTURY

AUGUST 9TH

*Ave Regina, pure and loving / Most noble; Ave Maris Stella, / Ave, Dear Maid, / Moon where God took hiding.*

HUGO RAHNER

## AUGUST 10TH

*O Mother of God, we take refuge under the protection of your motherly mercy. Despise not our fervent cries for help in the straits in which we find ourselves, but deliver us from all the dangers that threaten us, for you alone are the totally pure one, you alone are the truly blessed one. We make this plea, confident of your motherly compassion and relying on the infinite mercy that is your son. Amen.*

PRAYER TO OUR LADY OF LA SALETTE, 1846

## AUGUST 11TH

*Holy Mary, pierce me through / In my heart each wound renew / Of my Savior crucified.*

TRADITIONAL POPULAR PRAYER, FRANCE

## AUGUST 12TH

*We fly to your patronage, / O Holy Mother of God, / Despise not our petitions in our difficulties / But deliver us always from all dangers, / O Glorious and Blessed Virgin.*

SUB TUUM, THIRD CENTURY, CONSIDERED THE OLDEST
MARIAN PRAYER AND THE FIRST FORM OF HAIL MARY

*Queen of Angels,*
*Queen of Prophets,*
*Queen of Martyrs,*
*Queen of Virgins,*
*Queen of Peace,*
*Pray for us.*

LITANY OF LORETO

ADY *of Heaven,*

*Regent of the World,*
*Empress of the Marshes of Hell,*
*Receive me,*
*Your humble Christian;*
*Tell your Son*
*That I am his;*
*Ask him to absolve me*
*Of my sins.*

FRANCOIS VILLON

AUGUST 15TH *Feast of the Assumption*

Hail Mary, full of grace,

The Lord is with thee.

Blessed art thou among women,

And blessed is the fruit of thy womb, Jesus.

Holy Mary, Mother of God,

Pray for us sinners,

Now and at the hour of our death.

Amen.

TRADITIONAL HAIL MARY

## AUGUST 16TH

*When the most wise Virgin, who birthed Joy in the world, went above all the spheres and left the stars beneath her shining feet in gleaming radiant light, she was surrounded by the nine-fold ranks and received by the nine hierarchies. She, the friend of suppliants, stood before the face of the supreme God. You who inhabit eternally the dazzling lights of heaven—you archangels, you leaders of the spirits and angels, you thrones of princes, holy armies and powers, you dominions of heaven, fiery cherubim and seraphim, created from the Word—say whether such a feeling of joy has ever overwhelmed you as when you saw the assembly of the Mother of the Everlasting Almighty! O Queen, omnipotent in heaven and on land and sea, O Glorious Tender Queen, pray for us now and always, and raise us up into your glory!*

ADAPTED FROM THE RENAISSANCE LATIN HYMN TO THE VIRGIN, VIRGO PRUDENTISSIMA

## AUGUST 17TH

*All Hail, you who are everywhere known / For all angelic virtues, / Whose Assumption was the glorification / Of the whole human race and creation. / O Mother of God, remember me!*

ADAPTED FROM THE LATIN HYMN TO THE VIRGIN, O PRAECLARA OMNIBUS

### AUGUST 18TH

*Virgin marvelous, / Who did bear God's son for us, / Worthless is my tongue and weak / Of your holiness to speak. / Heaven and earth and all that is, / Thrilled today with ecstasies, / Chanting glory unto thee.*

SAINT EPHREM

### AUGUST 19TH

*Mirror of Justice, / Seat of Wisdom, / Vessel of Honor, / Cause of our Joy, / Mystical Rose, / Pray for us.*

LITANY OF LORETO

### AUGUST 20TH

*No peace can last without you, no hope for any work can be fulfilled without you; no safety for our homes can remain or for our world, no shelter for any of our possessions of which you, O Queen, are the most precious; Mother of God, watch always over all things and, with a glad smile, embolden the just, feed them your sweet honey, seat them at all moments at the Feast of God.*

ADAPTED FROM THE MEDIEVAL HYMN,
INTEMERATA DEI MATER

AUGUST 21ST

Hail Holy Mother enthroned above, O Maria

Hail Mother of Mercy and of Love, O Maria,

Our life, our sweetness here below, O Maria,

Our hope in sorrow, O Maria,

Turn then most gracious advocate, O Maria,

Toward us thine eyes compassionate, O Maria.

SALVE REGINA

### August 22nd *Feast of the Queenship of Mary*

*O Mary, conceived without sin, pray for us who have recourse to you. We are your children committed to your care by your son in his dying hour. Now that you are in heaven, we pray that you continue your manifold intercession on our behalf and bring us the gifts of eternal salvation. Amen.*

PRAYER TO OUR LADY OF GRACE

### August 23rd

*Rejoice, Mary full of grace. You are called and really are the most gracious of all joys, for from you was born the Eternal Joy and the vanquisher of our grief! Rejoice, paradise more blessed than the Garden of Eden, paradise in which are sprung up once more every plant of virtue and in which the tree of life has been revealed!*

SAINT THEODORE OF STUDIOS

### August 24th

*I invoke your royal name of Mary, / That is, sovereign Lady, / And beg of you with all my heart, / To admit me into the privileged circle of your family / As one of your servants, / To do your will, / As a humble slave and loving child.*

BARTOLOMEO DE LOS RIOS

AUGUST 25TH

Maiden-Mother, meek and mild,

Take, oh take me for thy child,

Ever-Virgin Mary throughout life, oh let it be

My sole joy to think of thee;

Ever-Virgin Mary!

CONCORDIA LAETITIAE

### AUGUST 26TH

EMEMBER, O most gracious Virgin of
Guadeloupe, that in your apparitions, you
promised to show pity and compassion to all
who, loving and trusting you, seek your help
and protection. Accordingly, listen now to our
supplications and grant us consolation and
relief. We are full of hope that, relying on your help,
nothing can trouble or affect us. As you have remained
with us through your marvelous image, so now obtain for
us the graces we need. Amen.

PRAYER TO OUR LADY OF GUADELOUPE

### AUGUST 27TH

*Praise to God, / To the most Glorious Virgin, / And to all the
Saints. / Most happy among women, / A Mother among
mothers, / A Virgin among virgins, / Mary Immaculate,
the ever Virgin, / To whom be praise and honor for
ever and ever.*

FERGAL DUBH O'GARA

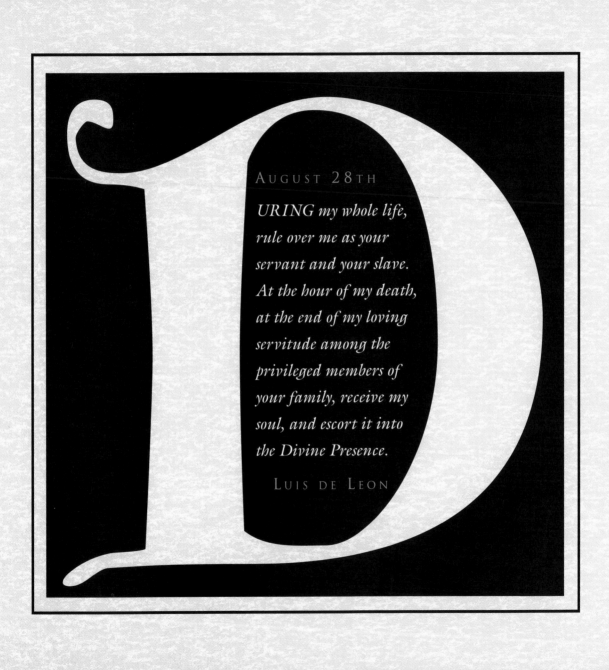

AUGUST 28TH

URING my whole life, rule over me as your servant and your slave. At the hour of my death, at the end of my loving servitude among the privileged members of your family, receive my soul, and escort it into the Divine Presence.

LUIS DE LEON

## AUGUST 29TH

*O Mother, I thank God for having given you, for my good, so sweet, so powerful, so lovely a name. But I will not be content with merely pronouncing your name; let my love for you prompt me ever to hail you, O Mother of Perpetual Help.*

PRAYER TO OUR LADY OF PERPETUAL HELP

## AUGUST 30TH

*Woman clothed with the sun, / Woman clothed with the stars, / Lady most benign, / Lady most merciful, / Our Lady, / Pray for us.*

LITANY OF LORETO

## AUGUST 31ST

*All-powerful and ever-living God, you raised the sinless Virgin Mary, mother of your son, body and soul to the glory of heaven. May we see heaven as our final goal and come to share her Glory.*

TRADITIONAL MASS OF THE ASSUMPTION

# September

## Mary in Islam

"When the Prophet of Allah
was cleansing the holy Kaaba
in the city of Divine Power,
clearing away primitive idols, he
allowed the beautiful fresco of the
Virgin Mary holding the Child
Jesus to remain, gracing the inner
wall of the inmost sanctuary of Islam,
just as the Virgin and her radiant child
remain central in Islam."

LEX HIXON, ATOM FROM THE
SUN OF KNOWLEDGE

*Few Christians know that Mary is also deeply venerated in Islam. I have dedicated the month of September to this veneration, in the hope that knowledge of it can soften and illumine the dialogue between the two religions, as well as extend our inner knowledge of the Mother.*

*Mary is, with Hadija and Asiya, wives of the Prophet, and Fatima, his daughter, one of the four women in whom Islamic tradition recognizes the "station" of perfection. Even at this degree of perfection, Mary enjoys a particular eminence, confirmed by the prophetic saying, "The highest of the women in the world is Mary; then Fatima, then Hadija, then Asiya."*

*Charles-Andre Gilis tells us in his definitive* Marie en Islam, *"According to the reality of her being, Mary manifests a fundamental aspect of the eternal word, expressed in the following statement of Allah, 'We have sent her as a mercy for the worlds' (*rahmatan-li-l-alamina*) (Koran, 21, 107). The 'divine mission' in question is underlined by the word* rahma, *which evokes the concept of 'matrix' and contains a distinct feminine and maternal connotation. From this, it is easy to understand that this 'function' includes in Islam an initiatory dimension, whose mysterious and rarely visible presence nevertheless manifests itself constantly." Elsewhere Gilis writes, "The majority of commentators on the Koran explain the meaning of the name Maryam [Mary] by the term* abida *[servant]. This term implies far more than external submission to the religion of Allah in its formal* and legal aspect. . . . In effect, the abida *isn't only the 'servant,' the one who has 'surrendered'; she is, above all, from the spiritual perspective, the 'one who adores purely,' the one whose inner and outer being are consecrated absolutely to God, destined for God, and purified by Him and for Him."* As Shaikh Hamid, a Sufi master, tells the protagonist in Reshad Feild's The Last Barrier, *"Mary is the Divine Mother, Mary is the blue of the flame, Mary is the matrix of all Divine possibility in Form, here in our world. It is necessary that she be recognized."*

In honor, then, of the Islamic tradition that so honors Mary, I suggest that this month you practice a simple and sublime Sufi heart-practice and consecrate it to Mary. The practice is designed to plunge the one who performs it into the Fire of the Heart, that Fire of Love that is Mary's essence.

First, invoke Mary the Mother and ask her help, so that the heart-practice can be as powerful as possible. Now, go deep into yourself to that solitary place in the heart which is peace, stillness, and love. This is the "virgin" space in the heart that no afflictions can destroy and no other loves can exploit. From this "virgin" space, an endless longing for the Divine keeps streaming.

When you have evoked for yourself this sacred space, imagine yourself seated in it, immersed wholly in, and surrounded on all sides by, a Sea of Light, the Light of the Heart of the Mother. Allow this Light to penetrate your whole being and body with its tender fire. Feel that not one part of your being—spiritual or physical—

*is outside this Love, not one toe or fingertip, not even the tiniest hair on your arms or legs.*

*You are now seated in her presence. Inevitably, thoughts, memories, and emotions of various kinds will arise. Try not to identify with any of them. As they arise, imagine that you reach out and grab hold of each of them and drown them one by one in the Sea of Love that surrounds you and that you are. In this way, you will merge them all with Love.*

*The feeling of Love is far more intensely dynamic than the thinking process, so if you do this practice with sincerity, all thoughts, memories, and emotions will gradually disappear. Nothing will remain. The mind will become one vast shining emptiness. You will become one with her Sacred Heart.*

*Rest in the Love you now are, her Love, as long as you can. As you begin to "surface" into ordinary consciousness, dedicate all the joy and gratitude you feel to the transformation of all beings throughout the universe.*

### SEPTEMBER 1ST

*There are as many paths to God as the children of God have breaths, but of all the paths to God, the Way of Mary, the Divine Mother, is the sweetest and most gentle.*

HAJJA MUHIBBA

### SEPTEMBER 2ND

*In every mosque in the world, the Mihrab, or prayer niche in the eastern wall of the mosque, is dedicated to the Virgin Mary. It is a shame that more Christians do not know this. Mary is the perfect woman, complete in herself, being the perfect matrix, the perfect receptacle from which Jesus could be born.*

SHAIKH HAMID

SEPTEMBER 3RD

*Before everything you possess vanishes, say to the forms of beings what Mary said to Gabriel: "I look for refuge from you in the All-Merciful."*

RUMI

SEPTEMBER 4TH

*The holy Mother was the stepping stone for Jesus toward Christhood.*

BOLAS

SEPTEMBER 5TH

*This body is like Mary, and each one of us has a Jesus inside him. If the pain appears, our Jesus will be born. If no pain arrives, Jesus will return to origin by the same secret way he came, and we will be deprived of him and reap no joy.*

RUMI

### SEPTEMBER 6TH

*As long as Mary did not feel the pain of childbirth, she did not go toward the tree of blessings. "The pangs of childbirth drew her to the trunk of the tree." Pain took her to the tree, and the barren tree bore fruit.*

RUMI

### SEPTEMBER 7TH

*In Jesus, we find the animating power of God's spirit made flesh through Mary and Gabriel. The life-giving breath, through which Jesus can revive the dead, is evidence of the mingling of the human and divine in the womb of Mother Mary.*

IBN ARABI

### SEPTEMBER 8TH  *Feast of the Nativity of the Virgin*

*Grieve not that Mary has gone; the light that Jesus heavenward bore—has come!*

RUMI

## SEPTEMBER 9TH

*The Universal Soul met a separate soul / And placed a pearl on her breast: / Through such a touch, the Soul, like Mary, / Became pregnant with a heart-ravishing messiah.*

RUMI

## SEPTEMBER 10TH

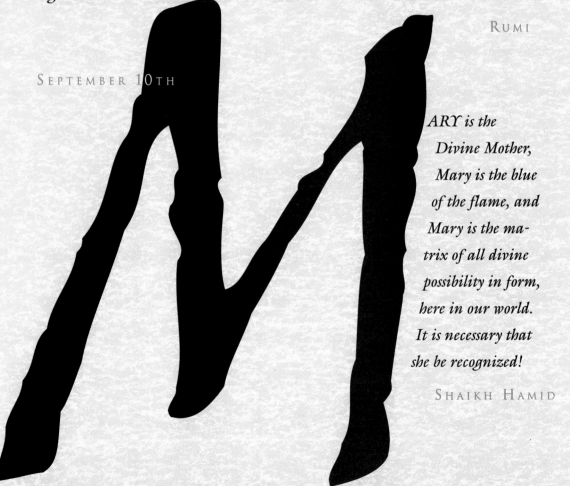

ARY is the Divine Mother, Mary is the blue of the flame, and Mary is the matrix of all divine possibility in form, here in our world. It is necessary that she be recognized!

SHAIKH HAMID

SEPTEMBER 11TH *Feast of the Glorious Cross of Mary*

*The Blessed Virgin Mary was chosen to bear the prophet Jesus because she kept her purity intact. Ordinary people refer to this as keeping her virginity, but those beings with the grace of deeper understanding know that to be pure means to flow completely with each moment, fully adaptable, to become like a ceaseless river, cascading from the very waters of life itself. To attain purity is to be a messenger that spreads joy through the world. Joy is the unfoldment of the knowledge of the perfection of God.*

RESHAD FEILD

SEPTEMBER 12TH

*Learn to love God with all your being, with every part of yourself, your heart, your mind, your soul, and then we all may be granted the meaning of the Virgin Birth. Learn to pray; and your prayers will come back from the very matrix that forms the Child.*

SHAIKH HAMID

### SEPTEMBER 13TH

*Sorrow for my Beloved's sake is a treasure in my heart; my heart is "Light upon Light," a beautiful Mary with Jesus in its womb.*

RUMI

### SEPTEMBER 14TH

*When the Angels in the Koran say to Mary that she has been chosen over all the women of the "worlds," the fact that "worlds" is plural shows the universal function of her presence.*

CHARLES-ANDRÉ GILIS

### SEPTEMBER 15TH  *Feast of Our Lady of Sorrows*

*And Mary, daughter of Imran, who kept her virginity, we have breathed into her our spirit and she embraced the truth of her Lord and his Book, and was numbered among those obedient to God.*

KORAN SURAT 66

### SEPTEMBER 16TH

*Mary said: "How shall a son be born to me, when no man has touched me?" He said: "Allah creates what he pleases; when he has decreed something, He only says to it BE, and it is."*

KORAN SURAT 4

### SEPTEMBER 17TH

*When the Divine Attributes of Creator and Reviver are manifest, they appear in the form of Jesus. When the Divine is manifested in the Attribute of Sustainer, it is expressed in the form of Mary following the Divine instruction: "And shake the trunk of the palm tree toward yourself, so that the ripened dates may fall for you, and you may take them for your sustenance." [Koran Surat 19]*

NAJIMO D-DIN RAZI

### SEPTEMBER 18TH

*Love is the Divine Mother's arms, and when those arms are outstretched, every soul falls into them.*

CHALAS

### SEPTEMBER 19TH

*When tomorrow, on Judgement Day, the cry goes out, O Men! the first person to step forward will be Mary, the Mother of Jesus.*

ATTAR

### SEPTEMBER 20TH

*The realization that belongs to Mary is that of* abida—*absolute servitude. Absolute servitude is not a "relation"; it is far higher than that; it is an unveiling and a state in itself. It corresponds, in fact, to the supreme descent of the Most High who takes the colors of His supports in order to become manifest, and this essential descent is the supreme secret of love.*

CHARLES-ANDRÉ GILIS

### SEPTEMBER 21ST

*Mary is identified with the Universal Koran, with the total manifestation of Divine Knowledge.*

CHARLES-ANDRÉ GILIS

SEPTEMBER 22ND

*He said: "It will be as it will be; your Lord says: It is easy to me. We will make your son a sign to men and a gift of mercy from us; we have decided and decreed this."*

KORAN SURAT 19

SEPTEMBER 23RD

*You are my children; All of you. Muslims, Christians, Jewish. And you are all brothers.*

OUR LADY, MEDJUGORGE, 1985

SEPTEMBER 24TH

*Insofar as she represents the origin of every conception and the limit of every under- standing, the Virgin appears as the Supreme Veil that Allah has descend between him and his servants. This Veil is one of mercy, with which he covers them and by which he graces them, according to their different needs and states, his protection and his forgiveness.*

CHARLES-ANDRÉ GILIS

SEPTEMBER 25TH

*This supreme veil that Mary is is not itself veiled from what it exteriorly hides from others: Mary, in her supreme perfection, is never for one moment in eternity separated from the glory of the Divine Essence.*

CHARLES-ANDRÉ GILIS

SEPTEMBER 26TH

*And she who had kept her virginity . . . We have breathed our Spirit into her. We have made of her and her son a sign to the world.*

KORAN SURAT 31

SEPTEMBER 27TH

*Without Love nothing in the world would have life.*
*How is an organic thing transformed into a plant?*
*How are plants sacrificed to become rich with spirit?*
*How is spirit sacrificed to become breath*
*One scent of which is potent enough to make Mary pregnant?*

RUMI

### SEPTEMBER 28TH

*When Mary's mother bore her, she made a vow to dedicate her daughter to the house of God and not to interfere in her upbringing in any way. So she left her in a corner of the temple. There she was found by the high priest Zachariah. . . . Every day, Zachariah would bring food to the child, and every day he would always find the exact replica of what he was bringing her in the same corner of the temple. He asked her, "Where do you get the other food?" Mary said, "Whenever I feel hungry, I ask God, and whatever I ask God, He sends. His generosity and compassion are infinite; whoever relies wholly on Him finds His help never fails!"*

RUMI

### SEPTEMBER 29TH

*Your son will speak to the world from the cradle, as a perfect adult, and he will be one of the shining ones.*

KORAN SURAT 4

### SEPTEMBER 30TH

*Paradise is at the feet of the Mothers.*

SACRED SAYING OF THE PROPHET

# Coming to Know Her Divine Radiance

Mary's mystical power, as Queen of Earth and Heaven and Mother of all beings of the universe, is infinite. This month I would like to invite you to practice a meditation I have found profoundly effective in contacting and grounding this power, which I have adapted from a Tibetan Buddhist practice. It has three stages: Invocation, Maturing and Deepening the Blessing, and Empowerment.

In the first stage, invoke in the sky in front of you that image of Mary that you love most. Try to imagine her as alive, and as radiant and translucent as a rainbow. Believe with your whole being that all the powers of the full Divine Mother are embodied in her. If you have difficulty imaging her, then simply visualize a Presence of Light, or just try to feel her presence there in the sky before you. The wonder and rapture that will then fill you can take the place of visualization.

Relax completely now and, filling your heart and mind with Mary's presence, invoke her with the full passion of your heart, calling out to her inwardly something like, "Mother, help me; help me dissolve the darkness in me and all the

# ctober

other habits that have bound me to ignorance. Help me to realize your peace and knowledge."

Then, with profound devotion, let your heart merge with her Sacred Heart. As you do so, give yourself up to her, saying inwardly something like, "Help me, Mother. Take complete care of me in every way. Fill me from the top of my head to the end of my toes with your joy and tenderness and energy. Fire my heart with your compassion; gather me into the heart of your wisdom." Know that when you call to Mary there is no doubt that the blessing you are praying for will enter your being. As you invoke her, your own inner Mary, the part of you that is forever one with her, will start to awaken and blossom naturally.

The next stage, Maturing and Deepening the Blessing, requires all the creativity of your open heart. Using a simple prayer to Mary that inspires you, go on offering your heart, soul, mind, and body in one-pointed devotion to her. Slowly, marvelously, you will feel your whole self coming closer to her and the gap between *you and her Peace-Mind growing less and less. Just as if you put your finger into water, it will get wet, and if you put it into fire, it will burn, so if you put your whole being into her, you will feel it transform into her being. Your ordinary mind and state of feeling dissolve, and your innermost love-nature, that is her Love-Nature, begins to unveil itself.*

*In the third stage, Empowerment, you open yourself completely to her mystic power, asking it to empower you in every way as her child. Imagine now that from Mary in front of you starts to stream thousands of brilliant white light rays. They emanate from her in a luminous torrent of light energy to purify, heal, and bless every part of you and to sow in your core the seeds of complete, conscious awakening into her.*

*When you have repeated the practice several times, rest in the peace it brings. With your heart now full of her love, dedicate everything you have felt and received to the awakening of all beings everywhere into their essential Love-Nature and to the coming of her Kingdom of Love on earth.*

OCTOBER 1ST

FOR *lofty fidelity is given charge*
*Over all who pass through humility*
*That she lead them without fail*
*To where Mary is one with Love in all.*

HADEWIJCH OF ANTWERP

OCTOBER 2ND

*She is more beautiful than the sun, and above all the order of stars: being compared with light, she is found before it.*

WISDOM 7:7

## OCTOBER 3RD

*I beg you never ever to be ungrateful to the Holy Virgin: she cares so deeply for you.*

ANGELA OF FOLIGNO

## OCTOBER 4TH

*Then the scholars and the Pharisees said, "Are you the mother of this child?" And she said, "Yes, I am." And they said to her, "You more than any woman are to be congratulated, for God has blessed the fruit of your womb! For we've never seen nor heard such glory and such virtue and wisdom."*

GOSPEL OF THOMAS 19:9–13

## OCTOBER 5TH

*O gracious Queen, heal, I beg of you, my wounded heart.*
*Despairing, I come to you, confiding in you alone.*
*Without your help, I am ashes.*

JACOPONE DA TODI

OCTOBER 6TH

*Consider therefore how great was my suffering at the death of my son, and it will not be hard, when the time comes, to give up the world.*

OUR LADY TO SAINT BRIDGET OF SWEDEN

OCTOBER 7TH *Feast of Our Lady of the Rosary*

*I loved her, and sought her out from my youth, I desired to make her my spouse and I was a lover of her beauty.*

WISDOM 8:2

OCTOBER 8TH

*It is because humility of heart is the root and guardian of all the other virtues that the Virgin Mary, as if forgetting all the other virtues that flourished in her soul and body, commended herself only for humility and proclaimed it as the first reason why God was incarnated in her.*

ANGELA OF FOLIGNO

OCTOBER 9TH

*I will always give her thanks, / Whether I lose or win; / I will stand in her power.*

HADEWIJCH OF ANTWERP

OCTOBER 10TH

*Though still in chains*
*And baffled by the world's folly*
*And staggering beneath*
*The burden of matter*
*My soul saw your eternal splendor*
*And came to know your divine radiance.*

SOLOVIEV

OCTOBER 11TH  *Feast of the Holy Motherhood of Mary*

*God is sending you tests which you can overcome with prayer. God is testing you through your everyday work. Now pray that you may overcome every temptation peacefully.*

OUR LADY, MEDJUGORGE, 1984

### October 12th

*Who can put Mary's high honor into words? She is both Mother and Virgin. I am overwhelmed by the wonder of this miracle. Of course no one could be prevented from living in the house he had built himself, yet who would invite mockery by asking his own servant to become his mother?*

Saint Cyril of Alexandria

### October 13th

*She is the stem of the cluster of grapes,*
*She gave forth fruit beyond nature's means,*
*And he, though his nature bore no resemblance to her,*
*Put on her color and came forth from her.*

Saint Ephrem

### October 14th

*Do you seriously imagine that I possessed grace without effort? Know that I obtained no grace from God without immense effort, constant prayer, passionate desire...*

Our Lady to Saint Elizabeth of Hungary

### OCTOBER 15TH

*There is another supreme cure for all temptations:*
*vividly remember the purity and uprightness which*
*the Mother of God possessed with unique intensity.*

ANGELA OF FOLIGNO

### OCTOBER 16TH

*VIL spirits are terrified of the Queen of Heaven. They fly from the sound of her*
*name, as if from fire. At the very sound of the word Mary, they are*
*prostrated as if by thunder.*

THOMAS A. KEMPIS

### OCTOBER 17TH

*O glorious and happy faith!*
*O permanent and safe refuge from the storm of time!*
*The Mother of God is my mother!*

SAINT ANSELM

## OCTOBER 18TH

*She will take the racked treasure of our suffering on her knees and place it beside the tortured relic of Christ's body. Her arms contain all the suffering of the whole of humanity, the countless ever-growing number of wounds of a human race which is continuously crucified.*

EDWARD SCHILLEBEECKS

## OCTOBER 19TH

*God is still mysterious; he seems to have a precise kind of obscurity in store for each life but could he ever render any life as dark and incomprehensible as he did Mary's? "Blessed are you who have believed"—even when her faith became a sword that pierced her heart. The real reason for her greatness is this: She is the great believer.*

CARDINAL RATZINGER

## OCTOBER 20TH

*Lady, the price has been paid: He to whom you gave suck.*
*In the name of that filial love, turn to me.*
*Hurry, fragrant lily, hurry.*

JACOPONE DA TODI

## OCTOBER 21ST

*Until Mary*                    *had received love,*
                    *OVE first was wild and then was tame;*
                    *Mary gave us for the Lion a lamb.*
                    *She illuminated the darkness*
                    *That had been somber for long ages.*

                                    HADEWIJCH OF ANTWERP

## OCTOBER 22ND·

*None of my children is ever lost.*

            OUR LADY, MEDJUGORGE

## OCTOBER 23RD

*Her eyes are eyes of gentle pity, wondering sadness, and with something more in them, something which makes her younger than evil, younger than the race from which she sprang: although she is, by grace, Mother of the world, and Mother of grace, she is also our little youngest sister.*

                                    GEORGES BERNANOS

### OCTOBER 24TH

*From the beginning, the Virgin represents us all in her person. It is as if God awaited in her the response of that humanity to which he wills to unite himself.*

DOM COLOMBA MARMION (D.1923)

### OCTOBER 25TH

*You found grace and how vast a grace it was! So vast it utterly filled you. And this fullness was so immense it continues to pour down like a torrent on every living being.*

SAINT PETER CHRYSOSTOM

### OCTOBER 26TH

*As my Sovereign and my Queen,*
*Preside over all my actions,*
*Direct all my enterprises,*
*Remedy all their defects.*

BARTOLOMEO DE LOS RIOS

### OCTOBER 27TH

*Mother of all pots and pans and things,*
*Since I've no time to be a saint,*
*By doing holy things,*
*Make me a saint by getting*
*Meals and washing up the plates.*

SEEN IN A KITCHEN IN IRELAND

### OCTOBER 28TH

*When the world will end, then she will rest! But while the world is going on, she is so busy taking care of all of us!*

THE CURÉ OF ARS

### OCTOBER 29TH

*Having lost grace, the world is darker, the sun disappears, but the moon is still there for us. Let us address ourselves to Mary. Under her influence, thousands, every hour, find their way to Heaven.*

POPE INNOCENT III

Y

*You, O Lord, have given us in Mary arms that no force of war can annihilate.*

JAMES THE MONK

*Lift up your eyes from this dark epoch in which you are living and do not fear if, at present, Satan is uncontested ruler of the world and the Master of all humanity. Soon his reign will be reduced to ruin, and his power will be annihilated, because I myself will bind him with a chain.*

OUR LADY TO FATHER STEFANO GOBBI, 1992

# Giving Birth to a Miracle of Grace

As we approach the mystery of the Virgin Birth of Christ that is celebrated at Christmas, let us all remind ourselves of the profound meaning of this birth: that it must occur within us, at the very deepest level of our being. We are all called on to give birth to our divine selves in her and for her and through her grace.

Just as Mary the Virgin gave birth to Christ in history, so Mary the Mother gives birth to the Christ within each of us, to the sacred androgyne who we each essentially are, to the one who marries within himself or herself the "masculine" and the "feminine," to enter and embody a unity beyond either. This miraculous birth is what Christ is describing in *The Gospel of Thomas*: "When you make the two one, and when you make the inner as the outer and the outer as the inner, and the above as the below, and when you make the male and female into a single one, so that the male will not be male and the female not be female, then you shall enter the kingdom" (Logion 22).

# *ovember*

Such a birth into the kingdom of divine love and unity, as all serious mystics remind us (and as the alchemists who dived headlong into its mystery knew very well), cannot be anything but a long, hard, sometimes terrifying, sometimes completely bewildering process, since it involves nothing less than the subtle renovation of all our habits, the divinization of everything we are—of the mind as much as the heart, of the body as much as the soul. It demands a total commitment of our whole selves to her, so that she, with infinite, patient subtlety, can make pregnant with her grace the ground of our being, so that the birth into her can take place. Being reborn through this virgin birth in her means becoming a divine human child, consciously sustained at every moment and in every way by the Mother's love and the Mother's presence, released through the transformation of all inner darkness into a life lived purely for and in Divine Love.

This is, as mystics of every major tradition tell us, the highest, most mysterious, *and sweetest kind of rebirth. I believe that unless millions of us take this journey into rebirth-in-Mary, there will be no future. If we are as a human race to survive, it will be as humble, reverent, divine children of the Mother, reborn in her dimension, able at last to follow her guidance at every moment and so be directly empowered by her in the core of life with that vision, passion, stamina, and courage we need to change all existing conditions of life on earth for her, before it is too late.*

*As Mary said to a Swedish visionary of the twelfth century, Saint Bridget, "Dare to become my child by being reborn in the Fire of my Love and I will work the impossible through you daily."*

NOVEMBER 1ST

*For she is the brightness of the everlasting light, the unspotted mirror of the power of God, and the image of his goodness. . . . And being but one, she can do all things: and remaining herself, she maketh all things new; and in all ages entering into holy souls, she maketh them friends of God and prophets.*

WISDOM 7:7; 19:7

NOVEMBER 2ND *Feast of Our Lady of Grace*

*When Mary has put down her roots in a soul, she engenders there miracles of grace that she alone can work, for she alone is the fecund Virgin who has never had and never will have any equal in purity or fecundity.*

SAINT LOUIS-MARIE GRIGNION DE MONTFORT

NOVEMBER 3RD

*Already, thousands of hearts / Mary, are lifted up to you. / In their shadow-lives / They aspire only to you: / Radiant with future joy / They long to heal / O Holy creature / Pressed against your breast.*

NOVALIS

NOVEMBER 4TH

*Immaculate heart of Mary, ardent with your goodness, show your love toward us.*
*May the flame of your heart, O Mother, descend on all mankind.*

PRAYER DICTATED BY OUR LADY, MEDJUGORGE

NOVEMBER 5TH

*I must be the Virgin and give birth to God*
*Should I ever be graced divine beatitude.*

ANGELUS SILESIUS

NOVEMBER 6TH

*What does it matter to me if Gabriel salutes the Virgin*
*If he does not bring me the same news?*

ANGELUS SILESIUS

NOVEMBER 7TH

*The soul that's virginal, that conceives nothing but God*
*Can be pregnant with God as often as it wants.*

ANGELUS SILESIUS

In Mary,
man is married to GOD.
The male and the female unite in one person in an
interior marriage and the new man is born.
This is the mystery which has to be accomplished in us.
Every man and woman has to undergo this virgin
birth, to be married to God.

FATHER BEDE GRIFFITHS

### NOVEMBER 9TH

*Saint Augustine says that in this world, those who are destined for sanctity are all enclosed in the breast of Mary, and that they do not come out into the light until their marvelous Mother births them into Eternal Light. So, just as a child draws all its food from its mother, so those predestined for the divine life draw all their spiritual sustenance and all their strength from Mary.*

SAINT LOUIS-MARIE GRIGNION DE MONTFORT

### NOVEMBER 10TH

*God says to Mary: "Reproduce yourself in my chosen ones, so I can see in them with joy the roots of your invincible faith, of your profound humility, of your universal sacrifice, of your sublime prayer, of your ardent charity and strong hope, and of all your virtues."*

SAINT LOUIS-MARIE GRIGNION DE MONTFORT

## NOVEMBER 11TH

*When by an ineffable but absolutely authentic grace, the blessed and divine Mary is Queen in a soul, what miracle can she not do in it? Since she is the worker of great marvels, particularly in the inmost soul, she works there in secret, unknown even to that soul, who by too avid a knowing would destroy the beauty of her workings.*

SAINT LOUIS-MARIE GRIGNION DE MONTFORT

## NOVEMBER 12TH

*All God's children are worthy of paradise. I am the Queen of peace, I bring peace to my children who turn to me. I am the Mother of all people.*

OUR LADY, MEDJUGORGE

## NOVEMBER 13TH

*True Mother, true friend, true love, true mercy, may your son grant me by your true mercy his protection.*

TROUBADOUR PIERRE CARDENAL

NOVEMBER 14TH

*Her milk is the virginal pure essence of the divine life, through which death meets its defeat.*

JOHN OF GARLAND

NOVEMBER 15TH

*Beyond our physical and psychic being, we have to discover our spiritual being, our eternal ground, and there the mystery of love is fulfilled. Some may come to this interior marriage by way of exterior marriage, others are called by the way of virginity, but all alike have to experience the virgin birth, the marriage with God, before they can reach maturity.*

FATHER BEDE GRIFFITHS

NOVEMBER 16TH

*Light was like a harbinger / To that bright One to whom Mary gave birth, / For his conception was in the victory of light, / And his birth was at the victory of the Sun. / Blessed be the Conqueror!*

SAINT EPHREM

NOVEMBER 17TH   *Feast of the Visit of Our Lady to Elisabeth*

*O Virgin, how my powers lag and my eloquence fails me in the face of your excellence, your bliss, your sublimity and your glory. For whatever we think or say of you falls utterly short of the praise you deserve and is utterly outstripped by your blessedness.*

SAINT EPHREM

NOVEMBER 18TH

*My wound is unspeakable, my Lady,*
*and it festers.*
*URRY, help me. Suffering unravels me;*
*My pain swells to a height, wails.*

JACOPONE DA TODI

NOVEMBER 19TH

*O Blessed Mother of God*
*Open to us the gate of mercy:*
*For you are the salvation of the human race.*

SAINT JOHN DAMASCENE

NOVEMBER 20TH

*We go to heaven in full consciousness, as we are now. At the moment of the departure, we are aware of the separation of the body and the soul.*

OUR LADY, MEDJUGORGE, 1983

NOVEMBER 21ST *Feast of the Presentation of the Virgin in the Temple*

*O Mary,*
*I see this Word given to you*
*And not separated from the Father*
*Just as the word I have in my mind*
*Does not leave my heart*
*Or become separated from it*
*Even though that Word is externalized*
*And communicated to others . . .*

SAINT CATHERINE OF SIENNA

NOVEMBER 22ND

*Holy Mother, please fix the wounds of your son deeply in my heart. Grant me to be wounded by his sufferings, to be inebriated by his cross, for the love of your blessed son.*

JACOPONE DA TODI

### NOVEMBER 23RD

*Even the fallen Angels find grace in your eyes! O woman full and complete, pour your graces on this world and make all creatures green again.*

SAINT ANSELM

### NOVEMBER 24TH

*Don't be afflicted by suffering! I am here with you. Suffering is a test of a soul's faithfulness.*

OUR LADY, MEDJUGORGE

### NOVEMBER 25TH

*The most Holy Mother, who is the Mother of tenderness and mercy, and who never lets herself be outdone in love and liberality, when we give ourselves entirely to her, to honor and to serve her, and for that end strip ourselves of all that is dearest to us in order to adorn her, meets us in the same spirit.*

SAINT LOUIS-MARIE GRIGNION DE MONTFORT

## NOVEMBER 26TH

*Those who trust themselves to me through the rosary shall not perish. What you ask through a rosary, you will obtain.*

OUR LADY, MEDJUGORGE, 1984

## NOVEMBER 27TH

*Let her receive the King's diadem upon her head, as the Queen of Heaven, the Mother of all living, the health of the weak, the refuge of sinners, the comforter of the afflicted. And let the first amongst the King's princes walk before her, let angels and prophets and apostles and martyrs and all saints kiss the hem of her garment and rejoice under the shadow of her throne.*

CARDINAL NEWMAN

## NOVEMBER 28TH

*Our Mother, thou who art in the darkness of the underworld,*
*May the holiness of your name shine anew in our remembering.*
*May the breath of your awakening kingdom warm the hearts of all who wander*
    *homeless.*

PRAYER OF THE SOPHIA FOUNDATION OF NORTH AMERICA

### NOVEMBER 29TH

*I shall lead you as a guest from another country / To the chapel of the Inadvertent Joy, / Where pure gold domes will begin to shine for you, / And sleepless bells will start thundering. / There the Mother of God will drop her cloak upon you / From the crimson clouds; / And you will rise up, filled with wonderful powers.*

MARINA TSVETAYEVA

### NOVEMBER 30TH

*Anyone who knows Mary as Mother and submits to her and obeys her in all things will soon grow very rich; every day, he or she will amass treasures, by the secret power of her philosopher's stone.*

SAINT LOUIS-MARIE GRIGNION DE MONTFORT

# December

## Mary and Her Son Jesus

*Many years ago now, I visited Ephesus in Turkey and spent three days there worshipping in the small church on the hill near the house where Mary is said to have lived after the Crucifixion. I made friends with the old Jesuit who tended the shrine, and something he said has haunted me ever since. "Christ will come again," he said. "The Second Coming of Christ into the human mind and heart is certain. But it can only come, as it came the first time, through Mary. Mary is the key."*

*What these words now mean to me is that the human race will not be able to re-imagine the authentic Christ until it has faced and absorbed the full power and glory of the Sacred Feminine as incarnated in his Mother. Only then will it be able to recognize that Christ is as much the Son of the Mother as of the Father. Only then will it be able to realize that Christ's teaching of the Sacred Feminine—the greatest teaching, in fact, ever given humankind—is the "voicing" of the silence of the Mother as well as of the Father. Only then will it be able to see that Christ and Mary are one in the Fire of the Sacred Heart, and that it is the return of this Fire to the heart of every being that is meant by the Second Coming, and not some star-wars apparition of a Divine Avatar.*

*The "return" of Mary as the Divine Mother and of the power of the Sacred Feminine in general is crucial to the recognition of the full mystic Christ, and so of the full blazingly radical and transformative force of his mission and his love. The Mother and her Son came together to bring to humanity a path of Love-in-Action whose unsparing focus on justice would ensure that all conditions, spiritual and political, could be transformed into a living mirror of the love and justice of God. No path could be more demanding and more all-inclusive, and more dangerous to power of all kinds, including the power of all the established religions and churches. The Mother's passionate love for her creation and her Son's witnessing and enactment of that love are calling the human race to exert every effort of will and imagination to alter permanently the conditions of life on earth.*

*The very extent of the catastrophe we are living through makes it even more urgent that we take up their revolutionary challenge. Install Mary in the core of our being, and our inner Christ can be born; when each of our inner Christs are born, the Christ-consciousness can return everywhere, in a vast wave of divine passion. With that Christ-consciousness guiding and inspiring each of our decisions, private and political, ways will be found to eliminate global poverty, to unmake pollution of every kind, to protect and preserve nature.*

*Everything, then, now depends on how sincerely and wisely we turn to that Mother who can birth in us our own Christ Child in the most radical, humble love and commitment to enact that love in the world. As Louis-Marie Grignion de Montfort wrote, "For your Kingdom to come, O Lord, may the Kingdom of Mary come."*

### December 1st

*Mary is the personal subject of the humanity of Christ, and his feminine counterpart. To separate Christ from his Mother is, in effect, a violation of the mystery of Incarnation in its innermost sanctuary.*

Sergei Bulgakov

### December 2nd

*Our Lady's plan is a global plan that embraces every heart; it is the project of the triumph of her Immaculate Heart; to offer to her son the unity of our hearts for the salvation of the World.*

Bishop Hnilica

### December 3rd

*Jesus so lives in Mary that he is the soul of her soul, the spirit of her spirit, the heart of her heart. . . Jesus is so enshrined in the heart of Mary that in honoring and glorifying her heart, we honor and glorify Jesus Christ himself.*

John Eudes

## DECEMBER 4TH

*Until now, the divine Mary has been unknown, and this is one of the reasons why Jesus Christ is hardly known as he should be. If then, as is certain, the knowledge and reign of Jesus Christ arrive in the world, it will be a necessary consequence of the knowledge and reign of the Very Holy Virgin, who birthed him into this world the first time and will make him burst out everywhere the second.*

SAINT LOUIS-MARIE GRIGNION DE MONTFORT

## DECEMBER 5TH

*Whoever venerates her venerates me; whoever ignores her ignores me; whoever asks for anything from her has already received it . . . because she is my mother.*

JESUS TO MIRNA NAZOUR, 1987

## DECEMBER 6TH

*Pray, pray, pray! Pray continually! The heart of Mary and Jesus have merciful designs on you.*

THE ANGEL OF PEACE TO THE CHILDREN AT FATIMA, 1917

DECEMBER 7TH

*Look now on her who most resembles Christ*
*For only the great glory of her shining*
*Can purify your eyes to gaze on Christ.*

DANTE

DECEMBER 8TH *Feast of the Immaculate Conception*

*She gave birth to Christ twice: the second time was on the Calvary.*

THE CURÉ OF ARS

DECEMBER 9TH

*Jesus and I loved each other so tenderly on earth that we became one heart.*

OUR LADY TO SAINT BRIDGET

DECEMBER 10TH

*Come, eat my bread that is Jesus and drink the wine of his love that I have mixed with the milk of my breasts.*

OUR LADY TO SAINT LOUIS-MARIE GRIGNION DE MONTFORT

### DECEMBER 11TH

*By you we have access to the son, O Holy founder of grace and bearer of life and mother of our salvation: Grace now that we may realize him through you who through you was given to us.*

SAINT BERNARD OF CLAIRVAUX

### DECEMBER 12TH  *Feast of Our Lady of Guadaloupe*

*If I will to take myself dependent on the Mother, it is in order to become the slave of the Son.*

SAINT ILDEPHONSUS

### DECEMBER 13TH

*One reason why so few souls arrive at the fullness of the age of Christ is that Mary who is as profoundly as always the Mother of Jesus Christ and the fecund wife of the Holy Spirit has not been formed enough in their hearts.*

BOURDON

### DECEMBER 14TH

*When her beloved Son was*
*consummating the redemption of the world*
*on the altar of the cross, Mary stood by his*
*side, suffering and redeeming with him.*

POPE PIUS XI

### DECEMBER 15TH

*Mary is the treasurer whose treasure is* JESUS *Christ. It*
*is he himself whom she possesses, he himself* *whom she gives.*

EYMARD

### DECEMBER 16TH

*God has so closely united their two hearts that we can say*
*with truth that they are one . . . Because*
*they have always been animated with*
*the same spirit and filled with the*
*same sentiments and affections.*

JOHN EUDES

### DECEMBER 17TH

*The Spirit spread his wings / Over the Virgin's womb. / She conceived and gave birth / To the King of Kings. / With great power / She acquired him; / With thanksgiving / She loved him; / With complete tenderness / She guarded him; / With grandeur / She manifested him. / Allelluia!*

FROM THE ODES OF SOLOMON

### DECEMBER 18TH

*From her own flesh,*
*He received his flesh,*
*So he is called Son of God and of man.*

SAINT JOHN OF THE CROSS

### DECEMBER 19TH

*My mother must be accepted. My mother must be heard in the totality of her messages. The World must discover the richness she brings.*

JESUS TO GLADYS QUIROGA, 1987

### DECEMBER 20TH

*Mary, intercede with your son, as you did at Cana, so that we may receive the gift of the spirit and be transformed into the living Eucharist, radiating mercy. . . .*

FATHER GEORGE KOSICKI

### DECEMBER 21ST

*Mary is the dawn that precedes and reveals the Sun of Justice that is Jesus Christ . . . The difference between the first and second coming of Jesus will be that the first was secret and hidden, the second will be glorious and dazzling; both will be perfect, because both will come through Mary. This is a great and holy mystery that no one can understand: "Let all tongues fall silent."*

SAINT LOUIS-MARIE GRIGNION DE MONTFORT

### DECEMBER 22ND

*At the Nativity, she truly became the Mother of God because she gave birth to him; at the resurrection, however, she became the Mother of God by recovering what she had lost.*

DIONISIO VASQUEZ

### DECEMBER 23RD

*HE Angel said to her: Hail full of grace,
the Lord is with you; he is with you in your heart, with you in your belly,
with you in your womb, with you in help given. Christ the King has come
from Heaven, into your womb; therefore shall you be blessed among women,
for you have given birth to life for men and women alike.*

BLESSED RABANUS MAURUS

### DECEMBER 24TH

*As Scripture says, she named him Jesus; according to the Angel's explanation, it
means the one who will save his people from their sins.*

SAINT BEDE

### DECEMBER 25TH

*All things are now upended. The castle is a cave,
The crib a throne, the night engenders day,
The Virgin births a child. Reflect, O man, and say
Heart and mind must now be reversed in every way.*

ANGELUS SILESIUS

DECEMBER 26TH

OR your kingdom to come, O Lord, may the kingdom of Mary come.

SAINT LOUIS-
MARIE GRIGNION
DE MONTFORT

DECEMBER 27TH

*The time of my mother's victory is approaching.*

JESUS TO JULIA KIM,
KOREA, 1991

DECEMBER 28TH

*My father will have mercy on the world through the Immaculate Heart of my mother. My children, you too will see the glorious arrival of my Immaculate Mother.*

JESUS TO SISTER NATALIE, 1986

### DECEMBER 29TH

*Rejoice, depth hard to contemplate even for the eyes of angels!*

*Rejoice, you who are the King's throne!*

*Rejoice, you who bear Him who bears all!*

*Rejoice, star that causes the Sun to appear!*

*Rejoice, womb of the Divine Incarnation!*

*Rejoice, you through whom the creation becomes new!*

ROMANUS MELODOS, AKATHIST HYMN TO THE VIRGIN

### DECEMBER 30TH

*Jesus began and continued his miracles through Mary; and through Mary, he will continue enacting them until the end of time.*

SAINT LOUIS-MARIE GRIGNION DE MONTFORT

### DECEMBER 31ST

*Have confidence and hope. Have courage and patience. The hour of justice and of mercy has begun. Soon, you will see the wonder of the merciful love of the divine heart of Jesus and the triumph of my Immaculate Heart.*

OUR LADY TO ESTELA RUIZ, PHOENIX, 1992

*I*n your womb was rekindled that love
In whose warmth of Eternal Peace
This flower has come to blossom.

Here, in heaven, you are the noon-day blaze
Of charity, and, among humans below,
A brilliant always-dancing fountain of hope.

DANTE, PARADISO, CANTO 33


*I* see you in a thousand paintings
Mary, so tenderly depicted
Yet none of them can begin to show you
As my soul sees you.

All I know is that the world's chaos
Has suddenly dissolved, like a dream
And your heaven of unspeakable sweetness
Opens forever in my spirit.

NOVALIS

QUEST BOOKS
are published by
The Theosophical Society in America,
Wheaton, Illinois 60189-0270,
a branch of a world organization
dedicated to the promotion of the unity of
humanity and the encouragement of the study of
religion, philosophy, and science, to the end that
we may better understand ourselves and our place in
the universe. The Society stands for complete
freedom of individual search and belief.
For further information about its activities,
write or call 1-800-669-1571.

The Theosophical Publishing House
is aided by the generous support of
THE KERN FOUNDATION,
a trust established by Herbert A. Kern
and dedicated to Theosophical education.